Developing

READING AND WRITING

SKILLS

FOR THE YEAR 7 TESTS

CLARE CONSTANT · ANDREW BENNETT

Heinemann

Heinemann Educational Publishers
Halley Court, Jordan Hill, Oxford OX2 8EJ
A division of Reed Educational and Professional Publishing Ltd

OXFORD MELBOURNE AUCKLAND
JOHANNESBURG BLANTYRE GABORONE
IBADAN PORTSMOUTH (NH) USA CHICAGO

Text © Clare Constant and Andrew Bennett 2002

First published 2002
06 05 04 03 02
10 9 8 7 6 5 4 3 2 1

ISBN 0 435 10612 0

Designed and produced by Gecko Ltd, Bicester, Oxon

Printed and bound in Italy by Trento s.r.l.

Original illustrations © Heinemann Educational Publishers 2002

Illustrations by Abigail Conway: page 58, Beverly Curl: page 77, Karen Donnelly: page 23, Alice Englander: page 34, Martin Fish: pages 60, 119, Tony Forbes: page 25, Paul McCaffrey: page 7, Chris Molan: page 29, Nick Schon: pages 14, 71, John Storey: page 65, Gecko Ltd: pages 9, 24, 26, 32, 43, 89, 116.

Acknowledgements

Clare Constant would like to dedicate this book with love and thanks to D.G.

The authors and publishers would like to thank David Robinson for all his work as grammar consultant on this book, which is much appreciated. They would also like to thank the readers, and the schools at which material was trialled, for their invaluable feedback.

The publishers gratefully acknowledge the following for permission to reproduce copyright material. Every effort has been made to trace copyright holders, but in some cases has proved impossible. The publishers would be happy to hear from any copyright holder that has not been acknowledged.

Extracts: from *The Hatchet* by Gary Paulsen, published by Macmillan 1996. Reprinted by permission of the publishers; from 'Woman and Home' from *The Call and Other Stories* by Robert Westall, published by Puffin. Copyright © Robert Westall 1989. Reprinted by permission of Laura Cecil Literary Agency on behalf of the author's estate; *Cat in a Tumble Drier* by Jo Shapcott. Reprinted with the kind permission of the author; from 'I Spy' from *Collected Short Stories* by Graham Greene, published by Random House. Reprinted by permission of David Higham Associates Limited; *Sunsets* by Richard Aldington. Copyright © The Estate of Richard Aldington. Reprinted by permission of Rosica Colin Limited; from 'The Playground' from *Out of Bounds* by Beverley Naidoo (Puffin 2001) Copyright © Beverley Naidoo, 2001. Reprinted by permission of Penguin Books Limited; from *Skellig* by David Almond, published by Hodder & Stoughton. Reprinted by permission of the publishers; 'The Three Toed Sloth' from *Poems 1960-2000* by Fleur Adcock, published by Bloodaxe Books 2000. Reprinted by permission of the publishers; from *Catch* by Dennis Scott, from 'Colours of a New Day'. Copyright © Dennis Scott. Reprinted by permission of Joy R. Scott, Executor, Estate of Dennis C. Scott; from *The Sun - Hold Ye Front Page* by John Perry and Neil Roberts, News International 2000, published by HarperCollins Publishers. Reprinted by permission of HarperCollins Publishers Limited; from *Everyday Machines* by John Kelly. Text copyright © Marshall Editions Developments Limited. First published by Egmont Books Limited and used with permission; from *The Language of Genes* by Professor Steve Jones, published by HarperCollins Publishers. Reprinted by permission of the publishers; from *Buggin'You* by Jane Bolton/Jim-Bob Marsh, Meg@ *The Times*, 5th August, 2000. Copyright © Times Newspapers Limited, 5th August, 2000. Used with permission; from www.castleofspirits.com/shc.html. Reprinted with permission; from leaflet *Who Wants to be a Volunteer?* Produced by The Children's Society. www.the-childrens-society.org.uk. Reprinted with permission; Screengrab from www.comicrelief.com. Reprinted with permission; Leaflet *Is your name really Mum?* Reproduced with the kind permission of Oxfam; from *Born Free* by Joy Adamson. © Elsa Conservation Trust. Reprinted by permission of the Elsa Conservation Trust; Extract from 'The Making of Me' from *Echoes of War* by Robert Westall. Copyright © Robert Westall, 1989. Reprinted by permission of Laura Cecil Literary Agency on behalf of the author's estate; Extract from *Blitzcat* by Robert Westall, published by Macmillan Publishers. © Robert Westall. Reprinted by permission of the publishers; 'Terrorist' from *The Collected Poems 1955-1995* by Anne Stevenson, published by Bloodaxe Books, 2000. Copyright © Anne Stevenson. Reprinted by permission of the publishers; Extracts from *The Roses of No Man's Land* by Lyn MacDonald, published by Penguin Books, 1993. Copyright © Lyn MacDonald.

The publishers would like to thank the following for permission to reproduce photographs on the pages noted:

Cover: Image bank. Inside: Oxford Scientific Films (sloth, p52); Hulton Getty (Logie Baird, p70); Mary Evans Picture Library (Frances Galton, p80); Science Photo Library/Peter Menzel (girl eating insects, p84; baked tarantula, p85); Fortrean Picture Library/Larry E. Arnold (Mary Reeser case, p103).

Tel: 01865 888058 www.heinemann.co.uk

Introduction

Developing Reading and Writing Skills has been designed to help you develop successful reading and writing skills throughout Year 7. It will help you recognise your strengths and weaknesses at word, sentence and text level and pinpoint areas that you need to focus on for improvement. Using this book will ensure that your skills improve. It will also equip you with the knowledge you need for end-of-year assessment and beyond.

Section A enables you to use a number of *reading strategies* to develop understanding of a wide range of fiction and non-fiction texts, and to investigate their features and stylistic conventions. It then helps you to use what you have learned in order to *craft your own writing* successfully at word, sentence and text level, in different genres. The objectives for each unit are clearly stated so that you know exactly what you are learning, and the end of unit assessments help you to track your progress and set targets.

Section B gives you guidance and practice in preparation for the optional Year 7 tests. It is written by one of the leading developers of the tests. It contains:

- *guidance* that will help you to understand what the marker is looking for in different kinds of reading and writing questions, and how you can best respond
- *a diagnostic test* that will help you identify strengths and weaknesses early in Year 7 so that you can set targets and develop your skills
- *a practice reading and writing test* that will help you prepare for the actual test and give you confidence in your skills for end-of-year assessment and beyond.

Using this book will develop your reading and writing skills alongside thinking and learning strategies. This will help you in your work throughout Key Stage 3 and into the future. We hope that you enjoy using this book.

Clare Constant
Andrew Bennett

The following icons are used in this book:

 this is the starter activity   *this is the plenary activity*

 this is the main activity   *there are worksheets to support this activity*

The first three represent the different parts of the lesson structure.

Contents

Section B

Preparing for the Year 7 English test

A1 Reading and crafting stories

In this unit you will be developing the active reading skills you need in order to understand texts. You will also investigate how writers craft their stories so they achieve the effect on readers that they want. First you will look closely at a short story called *I Spy* by Graham Greene. Then you will go on to use some of the writing techniques he used as you craft your own story.

1.1 Active reading

Objectives:
- *working out what unfamiliar words in sentences mean*
- *developing key reading skills*
- *questioning a text, to help you understand it as you read it.*

Working out what unfamiliar words in sentences mean

1 Work in pairs and discuss ways you have found of solving this problem:

How do you work out what a word in a text means without using a dictionary?

As you may have realised, there are always clues to help you work out what a word in a text means.

First you need to think carefully about:

a) what the rest of the sentence and paragraph is about – read the sentences that come before and after the one with the unfamiliar word in it

b) whether there are parts of the word that you already know

c) what job the word is doing in the sentence, e.g. *it's an adjective describing the noun 'house'*.

Then you should try to re-write the unfamiliar word in your own words.

See how well you can do this by playing the following game.

2 **Beat the clock!**

Five of the words on page 8, in *I Spy* by Graham Greene, are in **bold**. Your teacher is going to read the page with you.

a) **Start the clock** when you reach a highlighted word. You have **sixty seconds** to read to the end of the sentence, and work out and write down the meaning of that word as it is used in its sentence.

b) **Stop**. Check whether you got the meaning right before continuing.

c) **Share**. What helped you work out the word's meaning correctly?

Practising key reading skills

Sometimes you might read a story, reach the end and still not know what the story is really about. You can make sure you understand a story while you read it by being an active reader. Below are four tips for active reading that you are going to try out when you read *I Spy* on page 8.

> **Active reading techniques**
> - **Predict**. Think about what you already know. Then work out what will happen next, e.g. *What is Charlie going to do?* You will need to check your ideas by spotting clues or details in the story which show you could be right.
> - **Visualise**. This means you picture the things you are reading about, e.g. *the characters, what happens to them, the places and things described*.
> - **Empathise**. You imagine what it must feel like to be the characters you are reading about and facing the same situations they are, e.g. *Charlie waiting in the dark*.
> - **Bring your own experience to bear**. Remember any situations you have been in, or read about, like the one you are reading about now and ask yourself: *What did that experience feel like? Why does this character feel the same (or differently)?*

3 The first paragraph of *I Spy* has been labelled with four thoughts (**A–D**) an active reader had while reading it. Decide which of the active reading techniques, described above, the reader was using during each thought.

4 Read the rest of the story. When you reach a **blue box,** stop and read the active reading tasks before reading on and searching for the answers.

B *Charlie is about to do something he doesn't want his mother to find out about.*

C *I imagine as Charlie waits he straining so hard to hear every sound that even everyday sounds like the waves o. the shore (which he is probably unaware of mos. of the time) stand out.*

D *When I've crept around the hous after everyone else is asleep it feels creepy but he's frightened. I wonder why?*

Charlie Stowe waited until he heard his mother snore before he got out of bed. Even then he moved with caution and tiptoed to the window. The front of the house was **irregular**, so that it was possible to see a light burning in his mother's room. But now all the windows were dark.
5 A searchlight passed across the sky, lighting the banks and **probing** the dark deep spaces between, seeking enemy airships. The wind blew from the sea, and Charlie Stowe could hear behind his mother's snores the beating of the waves. A draught through the cracks in the window-frame stirred his night-shirt. Charlie Stowe was frightened.

Practise predicting:
As you read the next paragraph decide:
- *What do you think Charlie is going to do?*
- *How has Graham Greene tried to hook his readers' attention so they will start trying to predict what will happen?*

10 But the thought of the tobacconist's shop which his father kept down a dozen wooden stairs drew him on. He was twelve years old, and already boys at the County School mocked him because he had never smoked a cigarette. The packets were piled twelve deep below, Gold Flake and Player's, De Reszke, Abdulla, Woodbines, and the little shop lay under a
15 thin haze of stale smoke which would completely disguise his crime. That it was a crime to steal some of his father's stock Charlie Stowe had no doubt, but he did not love his father; his father was unreal to him, a **wraith**, pale, thin, indefinite, who noticed him only **spasmodically** and left even punishment to his mother. For his mother he felt a passionate,
20 **demonstrative** love; her large boisterous presence and her noisy charity filled the world for him; from her speech he judged her the friend of everyone, from the rector's wife to the 'dear Queen', except the 'Huns', the monsters who lurked in Zeppelins in the clouds. But his father's affection and dislike were as indefinite as his movements. Tonight he had
25 said he would be in Norwich, and yet you never knew. Charlie Stowe had no sense of safety as he crept down the wooden stairs. When they creaked he clenched his fingers on the collar of his night-shirt.

Practise visualising:
• Read the next paragraph and decide whether this bird's-eye plan of the shop is correct.

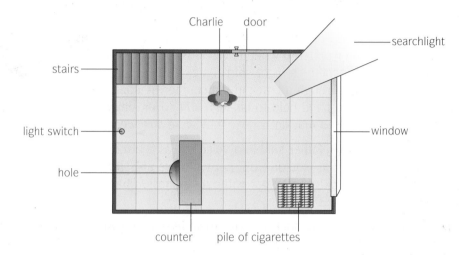

stairs

Charlie   door

searchlight

light switch

window

hole

counter   pile of cigarettes

• How has Graham Greene made sure his readers will have a strong idea of what the room is like in their minds?

At the bottom of the stairs he came out quite suddenly into the little shop. It was too dark to see his way, and he did not dare touch the switch. For
30 half a minute he sat in despair on the bottom step with his chin cupped in his hands. Then the regular movement of the searchlight was reflected through an upper window and the boy had time to fix in memory the pile of cigarettes, the counter, and the small hole under it. The footsteps of a policeman on the pavement made him grab the first packet to his hand
35 and dive for the hole. A light shone along the floor and a hand tried the door, then the footsteps passed on, and Charlie cowered in the darkness.

Practise your empathy skills:
As you read the next two paragraphs search for the answers
to these questions:
• How do Charlie's feelings change?
• How does the writer make sure readers notice Charlie's battle with fear?

At last he got his courage back by telling himself in his curiously adult way that if he were caught now there was nothing to be done about it, and he might as well have his smoke. He put a cigarette in his mouth and then
40 remembered that he had no matches. For a while he dared not move. Three times the searchlight lit the shop, as he muttered taunts and encouragements. 'May as well be hung for a sheep,' 'Cowardy, cowardy custard,' grown-up and childish exhortations oddly mixed.

But as he moved he heard footfalls in the street, the sound of several men
45 walking rapidly. Charlie Stowe was old enough to feel surprise that
anybody was about. The footsteps came nearer, stopped; a key was
turned in the shop door, a voice said: 'Let him in,' and then he heard his
father, 'If you wouldn't mind being quiet, gentlemen. I don't want to wake
up the family.' There was a note unfamiliar to Charlie in the undecided
50 voice. A torch flashed and the electric globe burst into blue light. The boy
held his breath; he wondered whether his father would hear his heart
beating, and he clutched his night-shirt tightly and prayed, 'O God, don't
let me be caught.' Through a crack in the counter he could see his father
where he stood, one hand held to his high stiff collar, between two men in
55 bowler hats and belted mackintoshes. They were strangers.

'Have a cigarette,' his father said in a voice dry as a biscuit. One of the
men shook his head. 'It wouldn't do, not when we are on duty. Thank you
all the same.' He spoke gently, but without kindness: Charlie Stowe
thought his father must be ill.

60 'Mind if I put a few in my pocket?' Mr Stowe asked, and when the man
nodded he lifted a pile of Gold Flake and Player's from a shelf and
caressed the packets with the tips of his fingers.

'Well,' he said, 'there's nothing to be done about it, and I may as well
have my smokes.' For a moment Charlie Stowe feared discovery, his father
65 stared round the shop so thoroughly; he might have been seeing it for the
first time. 'It's a good little business,' he said, 'for those that like it. The
wife will sell out, I suppose. Else the neighbours'll be wrecking it. Well,
you want to be off. A stitch in time. I'll get my coat.'

'One of us'll come with you, if you don't mind,' said the stranger gently.

70 'You needn't trouble. It's on the peg here. There, I'm all ready.'

The other man said in an embarrassed way, 'Don't you want to speak to
your wife?' The thin voice was decided, 'Not me. Never do today what
you can put off till tomorrow. She'll have her chance later, won't she?'

'Yes, yes,' one of the strangers said and he became very cheerful and
75 encouraging. 'Don't you worry too much. While there's life...' and
suddenly his father tried to laugh.

Bring your own experience to bear:
As you read this next paragraph remember a time when, like Charlie,
you learned something unexpected about someone close to you, and
answer these questions:

- Does Charlie react like you did? If not, in what way does he react
  differently?
- Why are readers likely to compare their experiences with Charlie's
  at this point in the story?

When the door had closed Charlie Stowe tiptoed upstairs and got into
bed. He wondered why his father had left the house again so late at night
and who the strangers were. Surprise and awe kept him for a little while
80 awake. It was as if a familiar photograph had stepped from the frame to
reproach him with neglect. He remembered how his father had held tight
to his collar and fortified himself with proverbs, and he thought for the
first time that, while his mother was boisterous and kindly, his father was
very like himself, doing things in the dark which frightened him. It would
85 have pleased him to go down to his father and tell him that he loved him,
but he could hear through the window the quick steps going away. He was
alone in the house with his mother, and he fell asleep.

*From **I Spy** by Graham Greene*

Now explain:
- *Which parts of the story have stuck in your mind?*
- *Why do you think this might be?*

How much did you understand?

The whole point of using active reading is to help you understand the story.
Find out how well you did this.

5   Work in a group. You have two minutes to tell your friends what
    happened in the story. If you hesitate for longer than five seconds, or get
    the story wrong, the first person to say 'BUZZ' scores a point and takes
    over the story telling.

6   As a class discuss how writers encourage their readers to read actively.

1.2   Reading between the lines

Objectives:
- *exploring how vocabulary choices create different effects*
- *examining the details in a text for sense and meaning*
- *understanding the way details in a text are used to give readers more information.*

Exploring how vocabulary choices create different effects

Graham Greene described Charlie's mother in a single sentence:

*her large **boisterous** presence and her noisy charity filled the world for him;*

Instead of 'boisterous' Greene could have used one of these synonyms
(a word that has the same or a similar meaning):

over-excited   hearty   restless   thunderous   frantic

1   Try placing each of the synonyms in Graham Greene's sentence. What difference does it make to what Charlie's mother is like? (You can use a dictionary to help you work out the answer.)

2   Work in groups. Decide how you can grade the words along a line going from the 'weakest' to the 'strongest'. Then add more synonyms to your line. (Using a thesaurus may help you gather a wider variety of words.)

3   a   Share the different ways in which groups have graded the synonyms. Then decide:

    b   Why is it important to think carefully about the meaning of the words that a writer has chosen to use?

Examining details for sense and meaning

I Spy focuses on Charlie, who is twelve years old and doesn't fully understand what is happening. To find out more than Charlie knows, readers have to think carefully about the details Graham Greene includes, and what these suggest. This sort of careful reading is sometimes called 'reading between the lines' or 'inference and deduction'. Below is one way to read sentences that carry extra meaning:

> **Reading between the lines**
> * *Pick out the **key words** – the words that carry the meaning in the sentence.*
> * ***Brainstorm** around the key words: what ideas does each suggest?*

4   Lines 11–13 describe something that has happened to Charlie before the story begins. Find out what else they can tell you using the reading technique above.

A *Why tell you his age?*

B *What does this suggest?*

He was twelve years old, and already boys at the County School mocked him because he had never smoked a cigarette.

C *What may be happening to Charlie?*

D *So what might he want to do?*

 5   Now practise using this technique yourself as you complete a chart like the one opposite. Read each span of lines and search for key words. Then discuss what these words or phrases suggest about the character.

Investigate	Line numbers	Key words	Inferences
Mr Stowe	23–25, 53–56, 60–64		
Charlie	15–19, 37–42, 79–86		
The strangers	54–58, 71–76		

6 Use all that you have thought about to help you:

   a) write a paragraph about each character describing what he or she is like

   b) suggest who the strangers were and what Mr Stowe might have been doing.

Explaining what you have learned

7 Your friends are missing this lesson and will need to catch up. Write them a **brief** note explaining one way they can 'read between the lines' of a story.

1.3   Planning a well-structured story

Objectives:
- *thinking up ideas for a story*
- *choosing the best idea*
- *turning your good idea into a well-planned story.*

Thinking up ideas for a story

1 Briefly share any ways you have found to solve this problem:

How do you come up with a *good* idea for a story *quickly*?

Since the first idea you think of might not always be the best idea you might have, it is worth thinking up several story ideas and then choosing the best from these.

This is one way of coming up with lots of story ideas to choose from:
- Look closely at the subject you are given (it may be a picture, a title or the first few lines). Spend a few minutes asking and re-asking yourself the same set of six questions (listed on page 14) to help you work out what your story could be about.
- Jot down every, and any, ideas you have, making sure you come up with a different set of answers each time.
- At this stage don't stop to decide whether the ideas are any good.

2   You have **five minutes** to think of as many ideas for a story as you can. It must be based on the picture below. Use a planning frame like this to jot down your ideas.

Questions	Story ideas 1	2	3...
1 Who?	Brother and sister	Friends	Enemies
2 Where?	In secondary school	At youth group	
3 When?	Summer term	Before Mum ...	
4 What?	Need to get camera mended		
5 Why?	So Mum won't find out		
6 How?	Earn money with homework writing service - but it goes wrong		

Choosing the best idea and turning it into a well-planned story

The best idea for your story will be one where:

- you know about the things you are writing about and can describe them well
- the story idea will keep your readers interested.

3   Discuss your story ideas with a friend and decide how you should rank your ideas (e.g. labelling your best idea A, your next best idea B, etc.).

Now your best story idea needs to be turned into a plot that will keep your readers hooked. This may sound difficult but in fact many writers use a simple five-stage Master Plot to turn their ideas into plots.

 4 Read the chart below which explains how a story moves through the five stages of the Master Plot. Then try using the Master Plot yourself as you decide how

    a) *I Spy*

    b) *Cinderella*

can be told, using each stage of the Master Plot in turn.

The five stages of the Master Plot	1 Exposition Tell when and where the story takes place and who it is about.	2 Complication The main character is faced with a problem.	3 Conflict Overcoming the problem makes life difficult.	4 Crisis Things become as bad as they can get.	5 Resolution Someone sorts the crisis out – happily or unhappily.
The plot of Red Riding Hood.	Once upon a time Red Riding Hood took some food to her Grandma's house because Grandma was ill in bed.	Red Riding Hood had to work out whether it really was Grandma in her bed, or a wolf who might eat her.	Red Riding Hood noticed what big ears and eyes this Grandma had. But the wolf kept trying to convince her he was Grandma.	Then Red Riding Hood said, 'What big teeth you have, Grandma' and the wolf said, 'All the better to eat you with!' Then he leapt at her.	Just in time the wood-cutter ran in and chopped off the wolf's head. Then they found the real Grandma in the cupboard and set her free.

5 Work in groups. Turn each person's best story idea into a plot that moves through each of the five stages of the Master Plot.

 Revising how to plot a story quickly

6 You have **sixty seconds** to explain to your friend how to think of a good idea for a story and turn it into a well-organised plot.

1.4 Writing your story

Objectives:
- *understanding past verb tenses*
- *managing verb tenses*
- *writing to keep your readers interested:* **show don't tell**.

Understanding verb tenses

1 Stories are usually written as if they happened in the past. How many ways can you write the verb *to walk* so it describes a past action?

2 The chart below explains how using different verb tenses can allow a writer to focus in different ways on particular moments to give them greater impact.

   a) Read the chart below, then search the lines in *I Spy* referred to in the charts and find the other examples asked for.

   b) Try to explain what effect the example of verb tense you found in *I Spy* has on the way that part of the story comes across to the reader.

Past perfect	Example: *Tess **had crept** up the stairs...*
	An event that took place before this moment in the story. Using this tense allows the writer to set the scene and create an atmosphere surrounding what is about to happen next.
	Find your own examples in lines 77–87.
Past continuous	Example: *and **was tiptoeing** along the corridor when...* (Note: this tense always contains **was** or **were**.)
	An action that carried on happening for a while. During the time it is happening another event (written in the simple past, see below) can take place (e.g. *when she heard...*). Using this tense can build a sense of excitement about what is about to happen.
	This tense is not used in I Spy.
Simple past	Example: *when **she heard**...*
	An event that happened at one particular moment in time. Using this tense after the past continuous can make the event sound sudden, which gives it more impact.
	Find your own examples in lines 1–2.
Present participle	Example: *she heard someone **creeping up** behind her.*
	The full verb in the clause must be in the past tense, then the present participle can make it seem as if a past action is happening right at that moment.
	Find your own examples in lines 4–6.

Managing verb tenses and keeping readers interested

3   Compare the way these two students have written the first part of
their story.
    a   Which do you prefer? Why?

*Events are
told rather
than shown.*

As Jamie tripped the camera fell and smashed and the
lens cracked.

*All verbs are
simple past tense.*

*riter has chosen
fferent verb
nses which help
show reader
e events
ppening.*

Jamie had tripped. The camera was flying out of his
hand. His ears strained. There was a sharp crash,
shattering his dream of winning first prize. The lens
had cracked.

*Events are seen
from Jamie's point
of view – we are
told how they
affect him.*

    b   Refer to the chart on page 16 to help you explain how the tense of
each verb (highlighted) helps the second writer show rather than just
tell readers what is happening.

4   Use what you have understood about the effect of using different verb
tenses to help you finish this next paragraph, making sure you:
    ● still show the story as it happens to, and affects, Jamie (his viewpoint)
    ● use three different verb tenses to express events happening.

*Jamie had just picked himself up off the floor and was bending over
the broken camera when he heard...*

5   Now use your plan and write the first three stages of your story.
Remember to:
    ● decide which character's viewpoint to tell the story from
    ● write in such a way that you show events happening
    ● choose the most effective verb tense(s) for each sentence.

Evaluating your choices

6   Read a friend's work. Choose the best paragraph and discuss:
    a) whether each choice of verb tense helps to show readers what
       is happening
    b) how you could change one verb tense to make the writing more effective.

1.5   Crafting your story

Objectives:
- *investigating main and subordinate clauses*
- *creating a feeling of suspense in your writing*
- *varying your choice of sentence structure*
- *choosing punctuation.*

Investigating main and subordinate clauses

1   Sort the texts below into two groups:

    A   those that make sense on their own (**main clauses**)

    B   those that do not make sense on their own (**subordinate clauses**)

1 Charlie Stowe wanted to steal some cigarettes

5 who was being bullied at school

2 while he was downstairs in the shop

6 he decided to steal the cigarettes from his father's shop

3 because Charlie did not love his father

7 while Charlie was hiding under the counter

4 something unexpected happened

8 who was accompanied by two strangers

9 his father returned

2   Investigate whether you can make a sentence by joining:

    a)   two texts from group B (the subordinate clauses).

    b)   two texts from group A (the main clauses).

    c)   one text from group A and one from B.

    You may add a connective (*and*, *because*) to build the sentence.

3   How many ways can you build a sentence just using texts 7, 8 and 9 (without adding any other words – not even connectives – but you can put one inside the other)? As you write:

- decide whether using a comma or pair of commas to separate a subordinate clause from the main clause will make the sentence easier to understand
- remember to end each of your sentences with a full stop.

4   Use all the texts (but no extra words) to build a series of sentences that re-tell the opening part of *I Spy*. Remember to use full stops and commas correctly.

Creating a feeling of suspense

5   Your writing will be more exciting to read if you can create a feeling of suspense. As you read the paragraph below decide how this student used each of the techniques listed below and try them out for yourself.

a) Use different types of sentence, e.g.:

- questions that make readers wonder what is going to happen
- an exclamation showing a character's strong feeling.

Re-write one sentence which would have more impact if it was (i) a question and re-write one which would have more impact as (ii) an exclamation.

b) Vary the length of your sentences, e.g.:

- Short sentences can be more abrupt and dramatic.
- Longer sentences showing a series of actions taking place one after another can make it seem as if events are happening quickly.

Re-write the third sentence as a series of tense, shorter sentences.

c) Position the subordinate clauses in your sentences. Try:

- beginning with the subordinate clause
- dropping the subordinate clause into the sentence.

i)   *Re-write the third sentence so it begins with the subordinate clause (highlighted).*

ii) *Re-write the second last sentence, changing the position of the subordinate clause.*

The repair shop shut at 5.30 p.m. Would he get there in time? Jamie's lungs ached as he sprinted down the art block corridor, thumped open the door, flew across the playground and yanked at the gate. It was locked. Jamie, who was only 1.2 metres tall, reached for its top bar and grasped the top of the gate for a few seconds. But then his fingers slipped and he dropped down. Unless there was another way out he would be locked in till morning. There had to be another way out.

6   Work in a group and write the next paragraph of the story using each of the techniques for creating suspense that you explored above at least once, e.g. *What about trying the...? As Jamie raced over to...*

7   Now write the crisis part of your own story giving it a strong feeling of suspense, before you go on to write your story's resolution.

Evaluating and improving writing

8   Read the crisis part of your friend's story and:

a) note two places where the feeling of suspense could be strengthened

b) discuss which techniques could improve these parts of the story

c) check that the story is written in whole sentences and make sure your commas help the reader make sense of different pieces of information.

Reading assignment

This test is 40 minutes long.

- *You should spend the first 5–10 minutes reading the text and questions carefully before you start writing your answers.*
- *Looking at the marks for each question should help you to judge how much to write for each answer.*

Brian is being taken in a small two-seater plane to visit his father when the pilot has a heart attack. Brian, who has never flown before, tries to land the plane.

The plane, committed now to landing, to crashing, fell into the wide place like a stone, and Brian eased back on the wheel and braced himself for the crash. But there was a tiny bit of speed left and when he pulled on the wheel the nose came up and he saw in front the blue of the lake and
5   at that instant the plane hit the trees.

There was a great wrenching as the wings caught the pines at the side of the clearing and broke back, ripping back just outside the main braces. Dust and dirt blew off the floor into his face so hard he thought there must have been some kind of explosion. He was momentarily blinded
10   and slammed forward in the seat, smashing his head on the wheel.

Then a wild crashing sound, ripping of metal, and the plane rolled to the right and blew through the trees, out over the water and down, down to slam into the lake, skip once on water as hard as concrete, water that tore the windscreen out and shattered the side windows, water that
15   drove him back into his seat. Somebody was screaming, screaming as the plane drove down into the water. Someone screamed tight animal screams of fear and pain and he did not know that it was his sound, that he roared against the water that took him and the plane still deeper, down into the water. He saw nothing but sensed blue, cold blue-green, and he raked at
20   the seatbelt catch, tore his nails loose on one hand. He ripped at it until it released and somehow – the water trying to kill him, to end him – somehow he pulled himself out of the shattered front window and clawed up into the blue, felt something hold him back, felt his anorak tear and he was free. Tearing free. Ripping free.

From **Hatchet** *by Gary Paulson*

1   Re-arrange the statements below so that they are in the same order as
    the plane's movements in the text. You need only write out the order of
    the letters.
    A The plane bounces on the surface of the lake.
    B The nose of the plane lifts so that it is no longer diving straight down.
    C The plane rolls over to the right.
    D The plane sinks into the water.
    E The plane has its wings ripped off as it crashes through
       some trees.

                                                                [5 marks]

2   What is the effect of the writer using present participles such
    as 'ripping' in the second and third paragraphs?

                                                                [2 marks]

3   Read lines 16–19. Which of the statements below best explains
    why Brian does not realise the screaming is 'his sound'?
    A Brian is unconscious.
    B Everything is happening so fast he cannot take it all in.
    C He has never heard himself scream like that before.
    D Brian cannot hear anything because he is under water.

                                                                [1 mark]

4   The whole of lines 11–15 is one sentence. How does
    the way the writer has built this sentence help show readers
    what the crash is like?

                                                                [6 marks]

5   How does the writer build a sense of suspense and tension in
    this passage?
    You should write about:
    • the way Brian flies the plane
    • what happens to Brian and the plane during the crash
    • Brian's struggle to escape
    • the variety of sentence structures the writer has used.

                                                                [10 marks]

A2 Exploring setting and character

In this unit you will investigate the effect of the details writers choose for descriptions of places and characters. To do this you will look closely at a room described by Robert Westall, and a character called Mrs Gamp created by Charles Dickens. Then you will try out some of their writing techniques in your own work.

2.1 Understanding how impressions are created

Objectives:
- *practising using a dictionary*
- *working out the exact meaning of a word in its sentence*
- *investigating the effect of the writer's choice of words*
- *investigating the impression created by the details used in a description*
- *investigating the impression created by varying the sentence structure.*

Investigating how a word is being used

Remember: when you need to work out the full meaning of a word in its sentence first think about what that word means and then what it suggests.

1 Sort the words in the box below into alphabetical order. Then use a dictionary to help you make a note of the exact definition of each word:

   quarrelling   intricate   devious   crude   rough

2 As you read the passage below find where each word is used and work out:
   a) what the word means in its sentence
   b) what impression each word gives of the thing it is describing. (See page 6 for a reminder of how to do this.)

A teenage boy is playing truant from school. The open front door of Miss Marriner's house tempted him to go in, but mysteriously the door locked itself behind him and now he is searching for a way out.

This was obviously the kitchen. Huge cold black kitchen range, and a battered electric cooker that must have been 1950s. Stone-flagged floor, with beetles scurrying away into the dark corners. The sink was full of dirty dishes, on to which the cold tap dripped, its sound quarrelling with the
5 ticking of the clock that had followed him in. Every work-surface was covered with an intricate clutter, like a spider's web to catch the eye. He got a feel of Miss Nadine Marriner's mind, somehow. A muddled, devious, cluttered mind. He didn't like it. His mum kept their kitchen spotlessly tidy.

But the huge pine table in the middle of the kitchen held different kinds of
10   things. A packet of cigarettes with one taken out, smoked, and left as a
trampled-out stub on the floor. A tin, with three crude rough-looking
cigarettes inside, that smelt funny when he sniffed them. Reefers?

A bottle of whisky, half-empty. And a glass with a thin damp brown stain
on the bottom.

15   He sniffed without touching. Yes, it was whisky all right.

Again he was tempted. But he'd tried whisky, and hated the taste. And his
first and only cigarette had made him sick. Besides, he didn't know where
they'd been.

He left them alone.

20   He looked under the table. There was a huge dirty bundle there: a
sleeping-bag wrapped round what looked like trousers and sweaters, with
an enamel mug attached by a length of coarse white string.

A tramp's bundle. A man-tramp, from the smell of it.

So now he had a tramp to worry about, as well. An old lady was one
25   thing. But a tramp who probably stole whisky and smoked reefers was a lot
more scary.

C'mon, let's get out of here. Quick. He moved swiftly to the kitchen door.
Undid the bolts, top and bottom. But it was locked as well, with a huge
old-fashioned lock. And the key wasn't in it. He searched the cluttered
30   work-surface in vain, feeling he was wasting time he could ill afford.

*From **Woman and Home** by Robert Westall*

Investigating how a writer has created an impression

Below is one way to examine a description thoroughly so that you notice what details the writer has chosen to mention, and can work out what they are showing you about that place or person.

 3 Make a numbered spider diagram like the one below. Then add notes to each of its legs in turn as you search through the passage picking out relevant details:

1

ORDER How does the writer organise the information?

Search through the passage and work out in what order the writer shows you the room: e.g. moving from near to far, up to down, or from the outer edge to the centre.

The first paragraph looks at the edges of the room. Then paragraph...

2

FIVE SENSES What clues are the five senses noticing?

Find sights, smells, tastes, sounds, things that are touched. Ask yourself: what impression do these give?

In line 4 the sound of the dripping tap is 'quarrelling' with the ticking of the clock. It creates a hostile atmosphere. You expect trouble!

7

SENTENCES How does the sort of sentences the writer used add to the mood?

Find and comment on examples of: a) some shorter sentences creating suspense, such as those in line 13 b) a long, detailed, complex sentence adding to the impression that the clutter was carefully placed, such as in lines 9-12.

Kitchen

3

FOCUS Which things are drawn to your attention?

Make a note of which things are described vividly or commented upon. Then try to work out why they are important – what do they suggest?

e.g. The cigarettes are drawn to our attention and the whisky because the boy examines them carefully. They are important because he is tempted to...

6

IMPORTANT Are there any hints from the writer about why this place is important?

e.g. Who does the kitchen tell you about?

4

VOCABULARY Think about the describing words the writer chose.

Pick out five adjectives, striking verbs or images. What does each mean or suggest?

e.g. In line 1 the kitchen range is described using the adjectives 'huge', 'cold' and 'black' which make it sound quite threatening.

5

CONTRAST Are any opposites being contrasted or similarities compared?

e.g. cold versus hot, dark versus light, or this kitchen versus a very different kitchen?

4 Think carefully about the different details you picked out and follow these steps to work out what impression all the details have built.

   a) Find any details that seem to link together, e.g. *clutter like 'a spider's web'* + *drink and cigarettes and drugs to 'tempt' him – like bait?*

   b) Suggest what impression these linked details suggest, e.g. *maybe it's a trap?*

   c) Search for any other details which agree or disagree with your idea, e.g. *Yes, he says Nadine Marriner's mind is... devious.*

Use a different colour to add these ideas to the edges of your spider diagram.

Examining descriptions

5 Without looking at your book or notes jot down the seven things you need to search for when you are trying to work out what a description is showing you.

2.2   Writing a description of a place

Objectives:
- *using a thesaurus*
- *choosing descriptive details that are relevant*

- *choosing descriptive details that create the right impression*
- *using prepositions and time and place conjunctions to build your description.*

Choosing descriptive details

1 You are going to write a description of the sort of house that might belong to this T.V. chef below. Each detail you put in should act as a clue showing readers what he is really like.

Eat only healthy food and you'll stay fit!

   a) Think up a name that suits the sort of person you think he is.

   b) Decide what impression you want to create as you describe his house, e.g. *The house belongs to a T.V. chef who is so in love with food that...*

   c) Spend two minutes brainstorming the sort of furniture and belongings a person like this would own, e.g. *sofas that look like cream cakes...*

Building detail into a description

2 You are going to write as if you have just walked into his house and are seeing it for the first time. Plan your description using a spider diagram like the one below. Make sure each detail you choose will act as a clue for your readers showing them what the owner of the house is really like.

1

ORDER *Work out the best order to write about what is in the house,*

e.g. If you want to show that he is a tidy person, go through each room in an orderly way starting with the nearest things first.

2

FIVE SENSES *Think of at least one clue about this person that each sense can give readers,*

e.g. Show how clean this TV chef is: does his kitchen smell stale (because there is mouldy cheese in the bin?) or of bleach?

7

SENTENCES *Which sort of sentence will you use to describe each room?*

A few short, dramatic sentences to make readers notice what is unusual or longer, complex sentences packing in details that build up a rich picture?

3

FOCUS *Which three things in the room should you draw your reader's attention to because they can create the right impression?*

e.g. The sofa in the lounge littered with books on healthy eating hiding burger and chip wrappers.

..........'s house. All details must create an impression of a person who...

6

IMPORTANT *Decide how you can hint about who this place tells your reader about,*

e.g. Rows of framed copies of magazine front pages, each with this personality's face under headings such as 'Health is happiness, says...'.

4

VOCABULARY *Which words or phrases will you use to describe things?*

*Find the best **adjectives** to describe each item, piece of furniture, etc*

e.g. so that the whole house sounds or looks like puddings: 'biscuit-coloured sofa smothered by a froth of creamy cushions'

5

CONTRAST *Choose one opposite you can use to contrast, or one similarity you can use to compare things,*

e.g. cold versus hot, dark versus light, stale versus fresh, this room versus a dieter's kitchen...

3 Work out where prepositions and time and place conjunctions (joining words) have been used to link the details in this student's description.
   1 Prepositions: *in, on, beside, against, before, under*
   2 Time conjunctions: *once, when, while, before, after, since, as, until*
   3 Place conjunctions: *where, wherever*

> As my feet sank into the strawberry-coloured carpet,
> I gazed around the room. Beside me a fudge-brown sofa
> lay smothered by a froth of cream cushions. Wherever I
> looked, photographs of Tofi Krisp beamed down at me.

4 a) How can you add or change details to make the sofa seem more like a delicious trifle? Write out your improved sentence(s).
   b) Add two sentences using prepositions to introduce descriptions of the lamps and ornaments making them seem like sweets.
   c) Add two more sentences using one time and one place conjunction to introduce descriptions of a coffee table and some bookshelves.

5 Now use what you have learned as you turn the ideas in your spider plan into a 150-word description of the house that the TV chef owns.

Thinking about detailed descriptions

6 Listen to your friends' descriptions.
   a) Raise your hand when you spot a detail that gives you a clue about the character. Be ready to explain what your friend did.
   b) Stand up when you spot a connective. Be ready to say whether it is a time or place connective.

2.3 Understanding characters

Objectives:
- *dealing with words in older texts that are no longer used*
- *discovering how punctuation of sentences has changed over time*
- *investigating how characters are revealed*
- *distinguishing the difference between a character's views and the author's.*

Investigating how to read older texts

1 Read the first paragraph of a passage written by Charles Dickens over one hundred years ago on page 29. Then think about any other stories written a long time ago that you have read (either in school or at home). Explain what you have found:
   a) interesting
   b) difficult about reading older texts.

- *You may not have recognised some of the words because they are not used regularly nowadays, either in conversation or in written texts.*

2   What can you do when there are words you do not recognise or understand? (See page 6 for help with this.)

- *You may also have found some of the sentences in the older text harder to understand. This is because we write sentences in a different way now.*

3   Compare the sentence in lines 8–14 of the text on pages 29–30 with the more modern version below. Find four differences in the way the two texts are organised and punctuated.

> *Mrs Gamp took Mr Chuffey by the collar of his coat. No doubt she intended to carry out the rules she enforced and 'bother the old wictim' in practice as well as in theory. She gave him some dozen or two hearty shakes backwards and forward in his chair. The disciples of the Prig school of nursing (who are very numerous among professional ladies) considered this exercise to be exceedingly helpful in restoring calm. Moreover they believed it to be highly beneficial to the performance of the nervous system.*

The differences you spotted are changes the writer made so that the passage could be more easily understood. They are things you can try when you need to make sense of an older text. Make a note of them as you complete this advice on what to do when you re-read a long sentence in an older text.

a) *Break it up into ___ sentences.*

b) *Find the main ___ in the sentence.*

c) *Move the position of other ____ so the sentence makes better sense to you.*

d) *Add p____ (e.g. separate chunks of meaning by using commas).*

By using these techniques to break it up more, the sentence becomes easier to understand.

4   Remember to follow this advice as you read the whole text on pages 29–30 and work out what it is about.

Investigating how characters are revealed

5   Spend a few minutes brainstorming lists of different ways writers can show you what a character in a story is like under these broad headings:

Description	Dialogue	Action
	e.g. what a character says, the way a character...	

6 Read the passage below and spot where the writer has used any of the ideas you thought of during your brainstorming. Note your ideas in a chart like this:

How the character is revealed	Examples from the passage	What it suggests about Mrs Gamp
Description Appearance:	red swollen nose, smells of spirits	suggests she drinks heavily
Dialogue		
Action		

Mrs Gamp is a nurse who sometimes looks after an elderly patient called Mr Chuffey. He has just become over-excited and Mr Chuffey's friend, Merry Chuzzlewit, is about to see how well Mrs Gamp cares for him.

The face of Mrs Gamp – the nose in particular – was somewhat red and swollen, and it was difficult to enjoy her society without becoming conscious of a strong smell of spirits.

'He's quiet now, Mrs Gamp,' said Merry Chuzzlewit. 'Don't disturb him.'

5   'Oh, bother the old wictim, Mrs Chuzzlewit,' replied that zealous lady, 'I ain't no patience with him. You give him his own way too much by half. A worritin' wexagious creetur!'

No doubt with the view of carrying out the **precepts** she enforced, and 'bothering the old wictim' in practice as well as in theory, Mrs Gamp took

10 him by the collar of his coat, and gave him some dozen or two hearty
shakes backward and forward in his chair; that exercise being considered
by the disciples of the Prig school of nursing (who are very numerous
among professional ladies) <u>as exceedingly conducive to repose, and highly
beneficial to the performance of the nervous functions</u>. Its effect in this
15 instance was to render the patient so giddy and addle-headed, that he could
say nothing more; which Mrs Gamp regarded as the triumph of her art.

'There!' she said, loosening the old man's cravat, **in consequence of his
being** rather black in the face, after this <u>scientific</u> treatment. 'Now, I hope,
you're easy in your mind. If you should turn at all faint we can soon rewive
20 you, sir, I promige you. Bite a person's thumbs, or turn their fingers the
wrong way,' said Mrs Gamp, smiling with the consciousness of at once
imparting pleasure and instruction to her **auditors**, 'and they comes to,
wonderful, Lord bless you!'

*From **Martin Chuzzlewit** by Charles Dickens*

precepts – rules
exceedingly conducive to repose – very good at helping patients to rest
in consequence of his being – because he was
auditors – the people listening to her

7 You are going to study lines 8–17 carefully as you discuss:

Does the writer agree with Mrs Gamp's ideas about nursing?

a) Start by thinking through:
  • What does Mrs Gamp think is a good way to nurse an upset patient?
  • How well is her patient, Mr Chuffey, after she has 'treated' him?

b) Then decide whether Mrs Gamp is what you (or any sensible reader)
   would expect a good nurse to be like.

c) Finally consider whether the writer expects readers to take seriously
   the underlined words that he uses to describe the ideas of the Prig
   school of nursing which Mrs Gamp follows. (For help with reading
   between the lines see page 11.)

Recognising how writers describe characters

8 Use what you have discovered in this unit to draw two memory maps
   (or spider diagrams) to help you remember the different ways:

a) a writer can show what a character is like

b) writers can show their true feelings about a character's ideas
   and behaviour.

2.4 Crafting characters

Objectives:
- *punctuating direct speech*
- *showing readers what a character is like*
- *exploring different types of subordinate clauses.*

Punctuating direct speech

1 Match each of these labels to its correct number in the passage below.

A *The speech must have punctuation before the speech marks close. If a full stop, question mark or exclamation mark is not needed then use a comma.*

B *Make sure it is clear who is speaking each time.*

When the next speaker speaks begin a new paragraph.

D *If the speech is introduced by some words like 'she said' then a comma is needed before opening the speech marks.*

E *A speech has to begin with a capital letter. The rest is punctuated like a normal sentence.*

F *The words which are spoken have to be written inside a pair of speech marks.*

> Kylie said, ¹'Mark, d'you know that shop, FitKits around the corner?'
>
> ⁵Mark growled, ³ '⁴Yes. ²'
>
> 'They've got some jogging bottoms. I'd love to wear a pair in purple and silver for the school cross country. I'm a size twelve,' she⁶ hinted.
>
> 'So?²' What was she telling him for? As if he was the slightest bit interested in the stupid race, the colours she liked, or her clothes size. Didn't she realise he hadn't got any money – she'd seen to that. Why wouldn't she leave him alone?

2 What order should these labels be in to form a list of instructions for punctuating direct speech? Write out the instructions, including examples from the passage.

Showing what characters are like

3 Read Kylie and Mark's conversation again. What clues does it give about:
   a) Kylie
   b) Mark
   c) how well they get on together?

4 Follow your rules and write five more lines of conversation in which Kylie persuades Mike to steal the clothes. (Keep them the same sort of people.)

5 Make a character wheel for Kylie, similar to the one below, which tells you what Mark is like. Choose details to show she is very different from Mark.

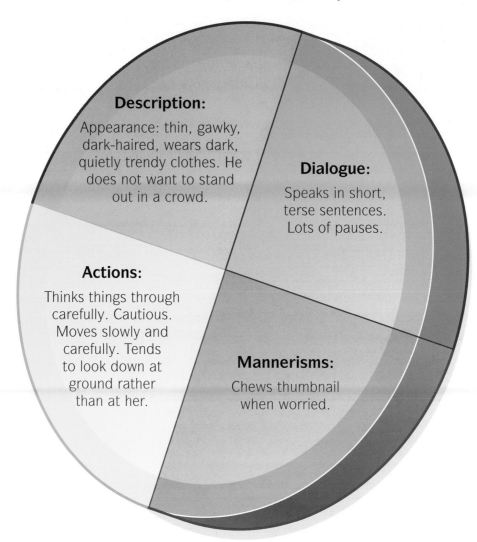

Description:

Appearance: thin, gawky, dark-haired, wears dark, quietly trendy clothes. He does not want to stand out in a crowd.

Dialogue:

Speaks in short, terse sentences. Lots of pauses.

Actions:

Thinks things through carefully. Cautious. Moves slowly and carefully. Tends to look down at ground rather than at her.

Mannerisms:

Chews thumbnail when worried.

6   Writers use different sorts of subordinate clauses to build different types of information into their writing. Decide whether each subordinate clause (in bold):

    a) tells the reader more about *what a person or object is like* (these relative clauses usually start with **which**, or **who**)

    b) gives more information about *the way someone is carrying out an action* (sometimes these adverbial clauses start with **as** or **when** or **while**).

> **As he chewed his thumb nail** *Mark stared through the window of FitKit. The jogging bottoms* **which Kylie wanted** *were at the front of the display. Mark took a deep breath, then,* **while pulling the grey hood down over his face**, *he shuffled into the shop,* **which was crowded with people**.

7   Now complete this paragraph using the two different types of subordinate clause to help you build in another detail about each word in bold:

> *As she was___(b)_____, Kylie* **wondered** *how Mark was getting on. 'There. Take it. Run!'* **Mark**, *who_____(a)_____, yelled and tossed a* **bundle**, ____(a)_____, *to her. ___(b)___ they* **ran** *towards the park.*

8   Mark took the wrong clothes. Finish the story, making sure you:
   - include details from Kylie's and Mark's character wheels
   - follow the rules for punctuating speech when you write any conversations
   - use the two sorts of subordinate clauses to add details to your description.

Tackling the problem of describing characters

9   What advice can you give this writer?

> Dear Tudor Penn,
>
> Please help. I'm writing this story about a teenager who cheats and lies to keep his place on the school football team. Can you give me some tips on the best ways to show my readers what he is like?
>
>   Yours,
>   A Harry Potter fan

Writing assignment

Minor task: you should spend about 25 minutes answering this question.

Your writing will be marked for:
- *your choice and use of vocabulary (4 marks)*
- *how you structure and punctuate sentences and organise paragraphs (4 marks)*
- *the overall impact of your writing on the reader (12 marks).*

Describe what is happening in this picture taking care to make the characters and setting as vivid as you can. You should aim to write about four paragraphs. Use a frame like the one below to help you plan your ideas:

Characters	1:	2:
Description e.g. Appearance		
Dialogue		
Action		
Setting		
Description		
Create suspense by		

Being able to read a poem you have never seen before and talk or write about what the writer has done is a real achievement. During the first part of this unit you are going to learn how to follow five simple steps that will help you explore any poem you read:

Step 1   Summarise the meaning
Step 2   Search for powerful words
Step 3   Look at the poem's images
Step 4   Listen to the poem's sound effects
Step 5   Notice how the poem is organised

You will practise using these steps as you read four very different poems by Jo Shapcott, the Dinka, Oscar Wilde and Richard Aldington. Later you will go on to use some of these poets' techniques in your own writing.

3.1   Beginning to explore a poem

Objectives:
- *using the right terminology*
- *investigating the impact of a writer's choice of words.*

Using the right terminology

It will help you talk and write about what a poet has achieved in a poem if you can use the correct terms to describe what the writer has done.

1   Here are eight technical terms whose meaning you should already know. As quickly as you can, match each term to its correct meaning, e.g. *1F*

Terms		Meanings
1 Alliteration	A	Non-human objects are given human emotions, motives or actions, e.g. *the door groaned on its hinges.*
2 Simile	B	Words which end with the same sound, e.g. *bread, head.*
3 Onomatopoeia	C	A powerful image where two objects are compared in such a way that one becomes the other, e.g. *his bag was a cemetery for pens, crisp packets...*
4 Personification	D	A word whose sound echoes its meaning, e.g. *rustle, pop.*

5 Repetition	E	An image where two objects are compared using the words *as* or *like*, e.g. *the goal lay before him like an open door.*
6 Rhyme	F	A phrase where words connected or near each other begin with the same sound, e.g. *sweeping across soft, silent sand.*
7 Metaphor	G	Lines have a pattern of heavy and light beats, e.g. *The grand old Duke of York.*
8 Rhythm	H	Words or phrases used more than once for effect, e.g. *he twisted and twisted and twisted the cap but it still didn't come off.*

2   Now search poems **A** and **B** on pages 38 and 39 to find your own example of each term.

Investigating a poet's ideas and word choices

> **Step 1** *Summarise the meaning*

Write a few sentences summarising what you think the poem is about.

As you read a new poem through several times, line by line and sentence by sentence, try to pin down what you think it is about. Remember you can always change or add to these ideas as you get to know the poem better.

Make sure you put in your summary:
- what you can easily understand the poem to be about, e.g. *a cat in a...*
- any feelings or mood you think the poem creates, e.g. *amusing... sad.*

3   Read poem **A** on page 38 and:
   a) decide how well each of the students below have summed up what it is about. Refer to the poem as you explain your ideas.
   b) write a better summary of what the poem is about.

> **A** This poem is warning pet owners about the danger of cats getting trapped in tumble driers. The cat is miserable. The poem is quite serious.

> **B** It describes a cat trying to tear up washing. It's written in a fun way.

> **C** The poem starts as a tumble drier starts turning and ends as the drier stops. The way it is written makes it fun.

4   Read poems **B** and **C** on pages 38–39 and write a summary of what each is about. In a group, share and discuss each of your summaries, and together write a summary of each poem to present to your class.

5   Work alone. Read poem **D** on page 39 and write a summary of it.

A Cat in the Tumble Drier

Oh Oh Oh
the drier's on the go
can't get out and
try to shout and
5 mouth full of fluff and
other stuff and
scrambling paws and
tea towel in my jaws and
vest round my tail and
10 start to **wail** and
tail round my ear and
drier up a gear and
ear caught up in claw and
see you through the door and
15 flannel round my leg and
I start to beg and
fur hot and **frizzy** and
head's gone **sizzle dizzy** and
you're there through the glass and
20 more hankies **whizz** past and
Oh Oh Oh
the drier starts to slow
my fur starts to **spark** and
the **pillow-cases bark** and
25 the **nightdress winks** and
the clean wash sinks
to a stop

by *Jo Shapcott*

> A verb that brings to life the cat's struggle to get a grip as it is tumbled around the drier with the clothes.

> The sound stands out because it rhymes with tail in lines 9 and 11.

C Symphony in Yellow

An omnibus across the bridge
   Crawls like a yellow butterfly,
   And, here and there, a passer-by
Shows like a restless **midge**.

5 Big barges full of yellow hay
   Are moored against the shadowy wharf,
   And, like a yellow silken scarf,
The thick fog hangs along the quay.

The yellow leaves begin to fade
10   And flutter from the Temple elms,
   And at my feet the pale green Thames
Lies like a **rod** of rippled jade.

by *Oscar Wilde*

B   The Magnificent Bull

My bull is white like the silver fish in the river
white like the **shimmering** crane bird on the river bank
white like fresh milk!
His roar is like the **thunder** to the Turkish
5   cannon on the steep shore.
My bull is dark like the raincloud in the storm.
He is like summer and winter.
Half of him is dark like the storm cloud,
half of him is light like sunshine.
10   His back shines like the morning star.
His brow is red like the beak of the Hornbill.
His forehead is like a **flag**, calling the people from
 a distance.
He resembles the rainbow.

15   I will water him at the river,
With my spear I shall drive my enemies.
Let them water their herds at the well;
the river belongs to me and my bull.
Drink, my bull, from the river; I am here
20   to guard you with my spear.

Traditional, the Dinka, Africa

D   Sunsets

The white body of the evening
Is torn into scarlet,
Slashed and gouged and seared
Into crimson,
5   And hung ironically
With garlands of mist.

And the wind
Blowing over London from Flanders*
Has a bitter taste.

by *Richard Aldington*

(* a First World War battlefield)

Step 2 *Search for powerful words*

Now it's time to read a poem slowly and carefully and pick out any words the writer used that you think are striking or vivid.

The sort of words you are looking for are single words or phrases that:
- tell of dramatic actions
- pinpoint what your senses might notice – smell, touch, sights etc.
- surprise you in some way.

The words you pick should make you think:

This fits here perfectly! or Why did the writer choose that word?

To help you work out what to say about each word you decide is powerful you need to think about:

- what job it is doing, e.g. *describing, naming, showing an action*
- what each word means and what ideas it suggests
- whether it stands out because one of the techniques you learned to spot at the beginning of this unit has been used to make it stand out, e.g. *it rhymes*.

6 Look at the words in **bold** in poem **A** and discuss:
   a) whether each word is a powerful one
   b) what makes those that are powerful stand out?

7 Work in a group. Read poems **B** and **C** and decide whether the three words in **bold** in each are the most powerful (if not, choose others). Then explain what makes each powerful word or phrase stand out.

8 Read poem **D** and choose three words you think are powerful. Then explain why each of them stands out.

Starting to look at a poem

9 You have **sixty seconds** to explain to a friend in as much detail as you can how to start trying to understand a poem you have not seen before.

3.2 Investigating a poem's culture and imagery

Objectives:
- *exploring a poem's period and culture*
- *thinking about the idea of literary heritage*
- *investigating the effect of imagery.*

Investigating the period or culture a poem belongs to

Writers live in a real place and at a particular time and this affects what they choose to put in a poem, e.g. *a Victorian writer from 1850 would not write about a tumble drier because the machine was not invented then.*

1 Make a timeline like the one below. Then:
  a) examine each of the poems **A**, **B**, **C** and **D** in turn, and write its title against the time you think it was written. Be ready to explain your decisions.
  b) add a label above each title to show which of these cultures it reveals and how you can tell:
    - Victorian England
    - a British soldier's home
    - an African tribesman's home
    - a modern British home.

Past	1800	1900	1914–1918	2000	Present
	Victorian		First World War		

2 Discuss why some writing such as poems **B**, **C** and **D** in this unit have been remembered and valued for many decades while other texts such as advertisement jingles or the opening song for a soap may not be valued for as long. Then decide whether in your own opinion poem **A** is likely to still be remembered in 100 years.

Step 3 *Look at the poem's images*

First you have to find the images in the poem, then you have to work out what each image is being used to show you.

3 Brainstorm:
  a) What is an image?
  b) What different sorts of images are there?
  (To get started look back at your answers to question 1 on page 36.)

Spotting an image

Images are a word or group of words that show readers that two different things are similar, e.g. *A writer might show you that the colour of autumn leaves is the same colour as the setting sun by writing: 'Autumn leaves orange as a sunset'.* Images can be written in several different ways:

> * In **personification** the words make readers notice that an object that is not alive is doing something similar to what a living human or animal does. So look out for verbs that show an object acting like a person (*the ball* **whistled** *past*) or an animal (*the engine* **hissed and growled**).

4 Search lines 21–27 in poem **A** to find two examples of personification.

> * In a **simile** the writer uses words such as **as** or **like** to explain what is similar about the two things that are being compared, e.g. *beads of dew* **shone like diamonds** – the way both things shine is similar. Making readers picture diamonds helps the writer point out how bright and sparkly the beads of dew are.
>
> Looking for the words **as** or **like** in a text will help you spot a simile *if* you also check that they are being used to compare two things.

5 Search poem **C** and find four similes.

> * In a **metaphor** the writer writes as if one object has *become* part of the other. The writer may leave readers to work out why the two objects are similar, e.g. **a snake tongue of lightning flickered** *across the sky* – The lightning is forked like a snake's tongue and it moves like it too.
>
> Looking for expressions like these in a text will help you spot metaphors:
> * '(*1st object*) **was/is** (*2nd object*)', e.g. *the* **darkness was a thick blanket** *comforting him*
> * '(*1st object*) **of** (*2nd object*)', e.g. *a* **rainbow of socks** *fell from his bag.*

6 Search the first stanza of poem **D** to find one metaphor.

7 Work in a group to discuss what sort of image each of these is:
   a) coiled springs of hair framed his face
   b) the stream chuckled all the way down the hill
   c) her pen leaked like a split hose
   d) a forest of hands.

Working out what an image is showing you

Once you have found an image, you need to work out what it is being used to emphasise. Drawing a diagram like this can help you understand the way an image works more clearly. Then ask yourself each of these questions:

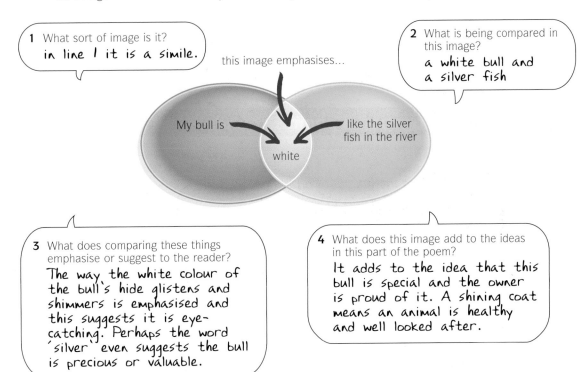

1 What sort of image is it?
in line 1 it is a simile.

2 What is being compared in this image?
a white bull and a silver fish

this image emphasises...

My bull is — white — like the silver fish in the river

3 What does comparing these things emphasise or suggest to the reader?
The way the white colour of the bull's hide glistens and shimmers is emphasised and this suggests it is eye-catching. Perhaps the word 'silver' even suggests the bull is precious or valuable.

4 What does this image add to the ideas in this part of the poem?
It adds to the idea that this bull is special and the owner is proud of it. A shining coat means an animal is healthy and well looked after.

ws 8 Below are diagrams to help you explore two more images from poem **B** (lines 3 and 6). For each one use the questions above to help you discuss what the image is showing you.

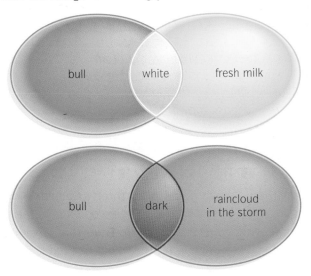

9 Work as a group to find and explore three other images in lines 2–12 of poem **B** using diagrams to help you. Share your ideas with the rest of your class.

10 On your own explore and explain the four images you found in poem **C**.

Exploring imagery

11 a) You have **sixty seconds** to explain clearly to a friend how to go about exploring the image expressed in the first stanza of poem **D**.

b) explore the image together, then share your ideas with your class.

3.3 Investigating a poem's sounds

Objectives:
- *understanding the impact of repetition*
- *investigating sound effects*
- *investigating a poem's form.*

Understanding the impact of repetition

A writer will repeat important words or phrases to make the reader take more notice of what they mean, or suggest, or what is happening.

1 You are going to use repetition to make your reading aloud of the four lines below sound more dramatic. As you look at each sentence decide:

a) Which is the best word to repeat? (try out different ones, for instance *beat* or *drum*)

b) How many times is it best to repeat that word (up to a maximum of four times), e.g. *Does saying 'The beat, beat of the drum...' sound more or less like the sound of drumming than 'The beat, beat, beat of the drum...'?*

c) Be ready to explain why you made your choices.

> *The beat of that drum is hammering my brain*
> *The crash of those cymbals is smashing my ears*
> *Your room shakes, simply earth-quakes*
> *Since I whispered, 'Please turn it down'.*

Investigating repetition and a poem's sounds

Look at the example opposite for one way to investigate repeated words:

 2 a) Work in a group. Search poem **A** for three examples of repetition and use the questions in the example to help you explore the effect of each.

b) Then work on your own. Search poem **B** for three examples of repetition and work out what the effect of each is.

A *Does the word or phrase mean and suggest the same thing each time?*

Both times it is the same cat's tail going round.

vest round my tail and
start to wail and
tail round my ear and

B *What does repeating it make readers notice?*

The cat is very aware of the different things happening to its tail: first it's caught up, then it is pulled about by the washing going round.

C *How does the repetition add to the ideas in those lines, or their mood?*

This repetition helps you picture the cat tumbling and tangling with the washing. Its tail goes round and round like the drier does.

3   As a class, make a chart of some of the different effects repetition can have using examples you made up earlier, and ones you have explored.

Step 4 *Listen to the poem's sound effects*

rhyme   **onomatopoeia**   **rhythm**   **alliteration**

4   Explain which of the sound effects above you would have found in the text if you had noticed:
   a) words describing sounds, e.g. *buzz, tick, sloshing*...
   b) words near each other beginning with the same letter or letters
   c) words near each other ending in the same sound, e.g. *tail, wail*...
   d) a line where the sound of the words has a regular beat.

When you notice a sound effect try to hear in your mind the sort of sound being created and ask yourself:
How does this sound effect add to the meaning of these words?

5   Which sound effect should each label point to in the example below?

A *The onomatopoeia adds to the idea that it's a harsh, unpleasant sound.*

¹The beat of that drum is hammering my brain.
The ²crash of those ³cymbals is ³smashing my ears.
Your room ⁴shakes, simply earth-⁴quakes.

C *The alliteration helps create the sound of the instrument.*

B *The rhythm of the line echoes the idea of the instrument banging away.*

D *The rhyme adds to the impression that the narrator is exaggerating.*

 6   **a)** As a group, find three sound effects in poem **A**. Then use the questions on the example above to help you discuss what effect each has.
   b) Work on your own as you find and explore three sound effects in poem **C**.
   c) As a class read poem **D** and discuss:
   • what sound effects are used
   • what effect each sound effect has.

Step 5 *Notice how the poem is organised (its form)*

Writers can organise their poems using these different patterns:

- **lines with the same pattern of beats and/or numbers of syllables**
  *Clap to the rhythm of beats in the first five lines of poem **A**,
  then count the number of beats in each line.*
- **stanzas with a regular number of lines and/or with a rhyme pattern**
  *Is the rhyme pattern in poem **C** always: a b a b?*
- **in sentences.**
  Which poems are written in sentences?

7 **a)** In groups look at poems **A**, **B** and **C** and decide which patterns
  are used.

  b) Work on your own to decide which patterns are used in poem **D**.

Once you have noticed that a pattern is being used to organise a poem
then look out for any places where:

- two patterns overlap, e.g. *a sentence and a stanza end together as in **C***
- the usual pattern is broken or changed, e.g *the first and last lines of **A***.

These places stand out and the meaning of the lines is emphasised, e.g.
*poets often use a change of stanza rhyme scheme as sentences end
and begin to emphasise that a new idea is being introduced, as in poem **C***.

8 As a class look at poem **B** carefully and decide:
  a) which pattern is being changed between lines 14 and 15?
  b) what change in idea is being emphasised by this change in pattern?

9 In groups look at poem **D** and discuss:
  - what change in idea is emphasised by the break between lines 6 and 7?

10 Look at poem **A** and explain how having a different rhythm for the first
  and last lines adds to the description of the tumble drier.

Remembering what to look for in a poem

11 Spend a minute explaining to a friend:
  a) what to think about when you are:
    - listening for sound effects
    - noticing patterns
  b) why you look for them.
  Hint: what does a writer use each of them for?

12 Make a mind map of the **five steps for reading a poem** you explored
  during this unit. Include brief details of how to follow each step.

3.4 Writing about a poem

Objectives:
- *including quotations in your work*
- *using terms to describe different effects in the poem*
- *writing about the way a poem is written*
- *working out what your personal view is, and expressing it clearly*
- *supporting your opinions using examples from the text.*

Including quotations in your work

When you write your review you will need to use quotations so that you can prove to your reader that your ideas are reasonable.

1   Read the rules for quoting and decide where each is used below:

A If you are copying more than a couple of words the quotation will have to begin a new line. It will need a colon to introduce it.

C You need to copy a poem exactly. Make sure you show where poetry lines begin and end, and what punctuation and spelling the writer used.

> At the beginning of the poem the writer says[1] :
> [2]'Oh Oh Oh
> [3]the drier's on the go'[2]
> to show the machine is starting to spin, and the repetition of the 'Oh...[4]' brings to life the surprise the cat feels at being caught in the machine.

B If you begin or end a quotation mid-line in the poem then use ellipsis (three dots...) to show this.

D The whole quotation needs to be placed inside quotation marks.

Writing a response to a poem

These five steps can also help you write a response to a poem:

Step 1   Summarise the meaning – *put this in your introduction*
Step 2   Search for powerful words
Step 3   Look at the poem's images
Step 4   Listen to the poem's sound effects
Step 5   Notice how the poem is organised

} – *write about each step explaining the examples you noticed and what effect each of them has*

2 Choose one of the poems, then work through the questions below to develop the thoughts you had about it into a well-organised response.

Planning your response

Introduction

A Say which poem you are going to write about and use the thoughts you came up with during **Step 1** to help you briefly sum up what it is about.

E.g. The poem I have chosen is 'Symphony in Yellow' by Oscar Wilde. It is about...

Main part of your response

B This is where you will write about what you discovered through following each of the other steps. Make a chart like the one below noting which quotations you will use:

	Example 1	*Effect it has*	*Example 2*	*Effect...etc.*
powerful words				
imagery				
sound effects				
patterns + how they change				

C Words like the ones in the box below will help you explain the effect of the examples you have picked out of the poem. Can you add any others?

Which...   suggests   implies   has the effect of
makes it sound like   also   because   in my opinion

Conclusion

D This is where you give your final opinion on what is most effective in the poem, and explain your reasons for thinking this.

E.g. I expected a poem called 'Symphony' to have lots of sound effects. However it was the way the writer used (e.g. imagery) that was most effective because...

3 Read the labelled example below. Work out the order in which the writer put:

a) the quotations

b) an introductory sentence to explain what the paragraph is about

c) a concluding sentence explaining what impact these images have

d) comments on what effect each image has.

The writer has followed the rules you learned to quote this image.

The poet used some surprising imagery in 'Symphony in Yellow'.
In the first stanza the moving bus is:
'Crawling like a yellow butterfly'.
This simile is striking because you usually think of butterflies fluttering, but the word 'crawling' shows how slowly the bus is moving.
Could it be that the butterfly bus is so loaded down with people it can't fly? Later a passer-by:
'Shows like a restless midge'.
Again the image of an insect is used but this time it is not as nice. A midge is usually a nuisance, which suggests the person spoils the scene the writer is looking at.
The poet seems to use the imagery in this stanza to show people can spoil things.

The writer doesn't always sound definite.

The writer points out what is similar about the two images.

The writer has compared the images and worked out what this might suggest.

4 Write a paragraph about the images in the second stanza, taking care to:

a) organise your writing in the same way as the example above

b) follow the rules for quoting.

 5 Now write your response using what you have learned.

Deciding what makes an effective response to a poem

6 Work in a group with others who wrote about the same poem as you. Read each other's response and decide which is most effective by giving grades A–C (with A as the best) for:

a) how well the poem is summarised in the introduction

b) whether good examples of each feature in the poem have been chosen

c) how clearly the effect of each example is explained

d) whether the final comments are explained clearly.

3.5 Using poetic techniques in your writing

Objectives:
- *expanding your descriptions*
- *using imagery*
- *describing an object, person or setting accurately and with impact*
- *using sound effects, rhythm, etc. in your writing.*

Expanding your descriptions

One of the things which made the poems interesting was that their writers found many different ways of describing things vividly. But sometimes it is hard to know how to fit more description in your writing.

1   Below are four labels explaining how a writer can fit more detail into a sentence. Match each label to its correct number in the following passage. (The words in **bold** are the **nouns** or **noun phrases** being described.)

A Add vivid **adjectives**: *think of what you can see, smell, taste and hear. These usually go before the noun and build a noun phrase.*

C Say **where,** *or* **when** *the noun occurs.*

B **Make a comparison**: *to show readers exactly what the most important feature of the noun is like. Write your comparison as a metaphor or simile.*

(Check back to page 42 for which words to use when writing your comparison either as a simile or metaphor.)

D Say how the noun **works** *or* **behaves** *(write this after the noun).*

> The word 'Dead!' struck **Rosa** as she drew ¹near the **cluster of children** ¹on the other side of the **fence**. She looked up and saw a boy pointing his forefinger at her through the ²**criss-cross wire fence**. He pulled his finger back sharply while his cheeks and lips exploded a short pistol blast. For a second she hesitated, her heart racing. She wanted to run. But that's what they were waiting for. Instead she forced herself to glance at all their faces. The narrow ³knife-grey **eyes** of Trigger-boy glinted with spite from under his ⁴**corn-tassel fringe**. But **the others** were more curious. ³Like cats hoping to play with a mouse.
>
> *From* **The Playground** *by Beverly Naidoo*

2   As a class try out these techniques yourself as you imagine Rosa's friend Mike arriving, carrying Trigger-boy's valuable watch.
   a) Use two adjectives to describe him *(he was…)*.
   b) Use a simile to describe Trigger's watch *(it shone like…)*.
   c) Say how Mike handles the watch *(tossing it? carrying it carefully?)*. Show Mike putting the watch somewhere out of Trigger's reach.
   d) Describe how Trigger looks as he sees what Mike does.

3   Now work on your own using each of the different ways of adding description to write the next paragraph describing how Mike uses the watch to help Rosa get away from the gang.

Using sound effects in your writing

4 David Almond describes an old garage in his novel *Skellig*, using some of the poetic techniques you investigated earlier (pages 36–37). Which of the techniques below does he use in the bold phrases?

rhythm   rhyme   alliteration   repetition   onomatopoeia

> *The door **creaked and cracked** for a moment before it was still. Dust poured through the torch beam. Something **scratched and scratched** in a corner...*
>
> *From **Skellig** by David Almond*

5 You are going to carry on describing the old garage, using sound effects to add to the impact of your description.

a) Brainstorm:
  - six different things someone might see in a garage
  - four sounds someone might hear, e.g. *water dripping, a mouse scratching...*

b) Then:
  - make a list of onomatopoeic words you can use to describe each sound, e.g. *rustle, thud...*
  - underline any words beginning with the same sound.

6 As you read the student's example below decide:

a) which words (perhaps verbs) the writer could repeat for more impact

b) how you could cut some of the words in the second sentence (highlighted) so that it is shorter and has a regular beat, building a feeling of tension.

> Cobwebs clung to my hair and drips of water splattered and splashed onto my hair. There was a scratch and a crunching sound, then a thud as a little mouse skittered across the floor in front of me.

7 Now write your own description of the garage using the ideas you thought of earlier and trying to use sound effects to bring it to life.

Using what you have learned

8 When you have finished your description, swap with a friend. Read each other's descriptions and decide whether you could improve it by:

a) putting in more details

b) using another poetic technique.

Reading assignment

This test is 40 minutes long.

- *You should spend the first 5–10 minutes reading the text and questions carefully before you start writing your answers.*
- *Looking at the marks for each question should help you to judge how much to write for each answer.*

Hint: Spend another 5–10 minutes using the five steps you learned in this unit to help you explore the poem before starting to answer the questions.

The Three-toed Sloth

The three-toed sloth is the slowest creature we know
for its size. It spends its life hanging upside-down
from a branch, its baby nestling on its breast.
It never cleans itself, but lets fungus grow
5   on its fur. The grin it wears, like an idiot clown,
proclaims the joys of a life which is one long rest.

The three-toed sloth is content. It doesn't care.
It moves **imperceptibly**, like the laziest snail
you ever saw blown up to the size of a sheep.
10 Disguised as a grey-green bough it dangles there
in the steamy Amazon jungle. That long-drawn
wail is its slow-motion sneeze. Then it falls asleep.

One cannot but envy such **torpor**. Its top speed,
when rushing to save its young, is a dramatic
15 fourteen feet* per minute, in a race with fate.
The puzzle is this, though: how did nature breed
a race so **determinedly unenergetic**?
What passion ever inspired a sloth to mate?

By Fleur Adcock   (*4.27 metres)

proclaims – announces
imperceptibly – so little that it is hard to notice
torpor – a lack of energy
determinedly unenergetic – thoroughly lacking in energy

1   Write down four facts you are told about this animal in the poem.
    [4 marks]

2   Find four words or phrases which help emphasise the slowness
    of the three-toed sloth in the poem. Explain why you chose
    each of them.
    [8 marks]

3   Which of the words below best describes how the writer views the
    three-toed sloth in the first two stanzas?
    annoying   boring   amusing   alarming
    Give reasons for your choice.
    [3 marks]

4   Look at lines 5–6.
    a) How does the length of the lines and the punctuation used affect
    the pace (speed) of these lines?
    b) Why might the author have wanted to create this effect?
    c) How does the image and use of sounds add to the impact
    of these lines?
    [5 marks]

5   How does the image in lines 8–9 add to the humour in
    these lines?
    [2 marks]

6   Which of these statements best explains why the author may have
    chosen the word 'dramatic' in line 14 to describe the sloth's turn
    of speed?
    A   The sloth is acting.
    B   This is a very fast speed so 'dramatic' emphasises how impressive
    it is to see the sloth moving this quickly.
    C   The writer uses 'dramatic' to add humour because this is a
    slow speed.
    [1 mark]

7   Re-read the last stanza.
    a) How does the way the writer thinks about the sloth change?
    b) What punctuation is used to show this?
    [2 marks]

A4 Experiencing drama

This unit helps you practise four steps that will help you understand any script. After you have tried out these steps on a script called *Catch* by Dennis Scott you will write instructions for how it should be staged.

4.1 First readings of a script

Objectives:
- *examining dialogue to understand characters*
- *exploring the impact of varying sentence structures*
- *thinking about the writer's choice of words*
- *making sense of character's actions*
- *making sense of events.*

Examining the way dialogue is written to understand characters

A scriptwriter does not tell actors much about the characters they are going to create; instead the script shows the characters speaking together and from that the actor has to work out what each character is feeling and how well they get on together. In the same way, you can work this out by looking at:

- what characters say – *the writer's choice of words*
- how sentences are punctuated – *questions, exclamations, ellipsis…*
- any stage directions – given in italics, and sometimes inside brackets.

1   Work in pairs. Prepare two readings of the script opposite: one reading following the instructions in A, the other following the instructions in B.

> A: Father is fed up and angry with his very young daughter. Read the script as if the adult is cross and the child is dreamy and childish.

> B: Mother and teenage son have had a wonderful time together. Read the script as if they are having fun joking with one another.

In front of a cage. Closing time at the zoo. It is obvious to the audience that the cage is empty. ¹ stage directions

PARENT: What's inside? (*Silence*)¹ Floor. Right. Flat. Nothing.² Nowhere to hide. Why are you doing this?³ Why you start lying like this?³

² short sentences

³ asking questions

³ asking questions

CHILD: If you look away quick, you can almost see him.

5 PARENT: Alright. (*Silence*) ⁷Get in. ⁷ commands

CHILD: No. Please.⁵ ⁵ choice of words

PARENT: ⁷Go on. It's alright, I'm here. ⁷ commands

CHILD: I don't want to.⁵

PARENT: I'll hold the door up and you slip inside. ⁵ choice of words

10 CHILD: It's... it's...⁴ ⁴ hesitating

PARENT: Just duck inside. You can walk all round inside, then you can stop pretending. Here. Mind your head! ⁶ exclaiming

⁴ hesitating

CHILD: I...⁴ I can't. He ... doesn't want me to.

2 **a)** Use the thinking frame below to help you work out how each of the labelled features suggests the script should really be read.

Language feature	suggests character is/feels	because...
I stage directions e.g. line 1	patient – feels in control	long break means you read it more slowly

b) Decide whether reading A or B suits the way the script is written. Use your thinking frame to help you give reasons for your decision.

Examining a script for meaning

3 Spend two minutes brainstorming everything you already know about the way plays are performed on stage, e.g. *actors...*

Step 1 *Making sense of action and events*

As you read a script make a note of what is happening and how each event helps build the tension that keeps the audience interested.

 4 Read lines 1–13 making a chart to show what happens:

lines	What happens?	How does this build tension?
1-10	Parent orders child to... Child doesn't want to	a disagreement – you wonder what will happen

5 Now use your chart to help you decide how well the script's ending suits what has gone before:

a) pick out any words or phrases in it that repeat what was said earlier

b) were you surprised by what happened or did you expect it? Why?

c) do you think the parent deserves what happens? Why?

Step 2 *Making sense of characters*

After you have read a script try to sum up in a few words what each character is like. Then test your ideas by searching it for evidence to back them up.

6 Divide into teams and read the part of the script printed on page 57. Then:

i) Each team jots down four words (a mixture of true and false) to sum up what each character is like (*tired, grumpy...*).

ii) Then each team swaps lists with another team.

iii) Each team must find a word or phrase in the text which correctly shows whether each word they have been given is true or false.

iv) The first team to find correct quotations for each of their words wins.

7 On your own, think about the whole script.

a) Can you tell what race or gender either character is from what they say?

b) How does this help or make things more difficult for a director?

c) Decide what age, race and gender each character would be if you were directing a performance of *Catch*.

d) Decide how you would want each character to look, using details from the text to back up your ideas, e.g. *The parent would be a... who looks well off...*

First readings of a script

8 Make a list of at least four keywords that will help you remember what to think about in each step when you first read a script.

	PARENT:	After three. Ready?
15	CHILD:	No. I won't.
	PARENT:	What?
	CHILD:	I won't do that.
	PARENT:	Because it's empty, right.
	CHILD:	I'm scared. He's... got big... hands.
20	PARENT:	Paws. People have hands. Animals have paws.
	CHILD:	I want to go.
	PARENT:	Not yet.
	CHILD:	The bell, you said it was for closing.
	PARENT:	Soon. Come. Inside.
25	CHILD:	No. No.
	PARENT:	One.
	CHILD:	Alright. It's true. It's empty.
	PARENT:	Two. I'm waiting.
	CHILD:	Just a joke, I'm sorry. It's empty. There's nothing, look, see?
30		I was joking –
	PARENT:	Three.
	CHILD:	Please don't make me.
	PARENT:	You have to learn the hard way. Alright. (*Hits* CHILD *deliberately three times*.)
35	CHILD:	(*Cries gently.*)
	PARENT:	Now, this is what I'm going to do. You listening? I'm going to lift that door myself, and I'm going to get inside, and I'm going to walk around in there, and you can see there's nothing there, there's nothing to be scared about, it's just your imagination, and then
40		you can shut up about things you can't see or hear and then we're going to go home, and I'm not taking you anywhere again you hear me? My child doesn't go on like that in public. Shut up and watch! (*Silence*) I'll give you something to cry about! (*Silence. Lifts the door, wriggles through the opening. The door drops behind him.*) You
45		see? Watch now, watch me, I'm inside, here, and I'm going to walk around, see. See? Nothing. Just a cage. That's that. And now we can go. Empty. (*Tries to lift door.*) I'm coming. Damn. (PARENT'S *nail is torn*.) Damn. Give me your handkerchief. Ugh. It's probably covered with germs. You brought a handkerchief?
50	CHILD:	(*Shakes head.*)
	PARENT:	Alright. I'm coming. (*Tries again. Stares at the door. Silence*) It's got an automatic catch. I think it's locked. Oh God... HELP! Quick, go get somebody. HELP! Move! It's your fault!

CHILD: (*Watches* PARENT.)

55   PARENT: Alright. Just go to – go and find the keeper, he'll have a key, just go now and we'll be out of here, and there's dinner waiting at home. (*Silence*) You heard me? (*Silence*) (*Quietly*) You're going to be very sorry, you're going to be very sorry when... HELP! (*Silence*) One. (*Silence*) Two. (*Silence*) Three. (*Silence*)

60   (*They stare at each other*)

CHILD: (*To self*) Closing time. (*Goes*)

PARENT: (*Looks at the cage. Hesitantly, nursing the injured hand, begins to explore it. Periodically, the hand hurts, and* PARENT *grunts a little in pain. Thinks.*)

Adapted from **Catch** *by Dennis Scott*

 ## 4.2   Reading between the lines of a script

Objectives:
- *investigating some differences between spoken and written English*
- *understanding the setting*
- *noticing the mood of a scene*
- *interpreting a script*
- *responding to the writer's choice of words.*

 ## Investigating some differences between written and spoken English

The way we speak and the way speech is written down are quite different. But do you know what the differences are?

1   Examine the speech in texts **A** and **B** (opposite). Find four differences between speech that is spoken and speech that is written down.

2   Now make a chart like the one opposite, showing the differences between speaking and writing speech in a piece of writing.

A A transcript of Lee Scott's actual words:

> '...I was trying to tell him... prove to him there wasn't anything in the cage so and I know this sounds stupid I got in... and and the door locked...'

B Newspaper article including speech:

> Yesterday a 30-year-old woman was found locked in a disused lion's cage at Wetchester Zoo. The woman, Lee Scott, said that she had got locked in while trying to prove to her toddler that the cage was empty. Andy Parks, the zoo keeper who released her, told us:
> 'People often say the animal accommodation in our zoo is as good as a hotel, but this is the first time anyone has taken a room for the night.'

Differences:	Spoken English	Written English
Hesitations	✓	✗

3   Is the way a script is written nearer to spoken or written English?

Preparing to perform

Unlike a novel or a poem, a play is **always** written to be performed. If it is a stage or television play, once you understand the characters and action the next step is to read it carefully and work out:

* how the text should be staged (costumes, lighting, set and props)
* what the overall mood of the play is.

Step 3 *Exploring the setting*

When you want to work out where a play is set search the script for clues to answer these questions:

* Where and when does the scene take place?
* How does the action of the play rely on where it is set?

4   Make a list of the clues in *Catch* that help you answer these questions, e.g. *The stage directions at... say... The action relies on the cage because...*

Step 4 *Noticing the mood*

* The mood of a scene makes an audience feel something, e.g. *they may feel fear if the mood of that part of the play is tense.*
* Mood is built up through the way the characters get on with each other and what is happening, e.g. *the sight of grieving characters at a funeral is likely to create a sad mood for the audience.*
* A director can make a mood stronger by changing the lighting and set design, e.g. *a dark set with gloomy lighting will add to a sad mood.*
* You can work out the mood of a scene by thinking about:
   i) what the audience is likely to feel as they see events happen
   ii) how the actors cause and respond to these events.

5 **a)** As you re-read lines 14–63 of *Catch* search for one clue that might suggest the child is imagining the parent and not an animal is trapped in the cage.

b) Are there other clues in the rest of the play that suggest the child is trying to trap the parent, or is it just luck that this is what happens?

c) How is the audience likely to feel about or respond to the parent getting trapped?

d) Now use what you have discovered to help you decide which of these words best describes the atmosphere or mood of *Catch*?:

tense   **light-hearted**   **sinister**   **calm**   **scary**

6 How could you use lighting and colours on the set that is on page 58 to help create the right time of day and mood in this part of the script?

 Remembering what to look for in a script ⓦ

7 Copy and add labels to this memory aid so that you will remember what to look for when you are reading a playscript (**ChASM**).

Characters

Look at (a) what they say, (b) how they say it (punctuation), and (c) stage directions

 4.3 Planning to write director's notes

You will need to refer to the notes you made earlier as you plan and write director's notes giving instructions to the team about to stage it.

Objectives:
- *writing in paragraphs using topic sentences*
- *reflecting on a script*
- *revising ways of planning your writing*
- *revising the features of an instruction text*
- *varying the formality of your English.*

Writing in paragraphs

1   Finish these sentences as you discuss how to write in paragraphs:

   a) Begin a new paragraph when you want to write about a new ___,
       e.g. ___.

   b) When you finish a paragraph leave a ___ before starting the next.

   c) Begin writing the new paragraph ___.

> *Catch* is an amusing short play by Dennis Scott showing what happens
> to one parent at the end of their visit to the zoo.
>
> The setting of the play is a zoo at closing time. The characters stand
> before a cage that is empty. The door to the cage is lifted up and the
> cage is large enough so that the child could fit in it quite easily, but the
> adult will have to crouch a little...

The first sentence of a paragraph is often called the **topic sentence**
because writers use it to tell readers what the paragraph is about.

2   Find the topic sentence in the example above. What does it suggest the
   rest of the paragraph is likely to be about?

WS 3   Work in a group.

   a) Use the questions in this thinking frame to help you discuss *Catch*.

   b) Copy out the frame and fill it with your ideas as you work out how
       to sort your ideas into three paragraphs.

*Think about each part of the play: Characters, Action,
Setting and Mood and decide what is effective about
each of them, and what is not so good.*

*Write a topic sentence
for each paragraph.*

Paragraph	Content	Topic sentence
1 What is Catch about?		
2 What are its strengths?	Characters are believable. The parent is so over-the-top angry you really enjoy it when s/he gets trapped.	
3 What are its weaknesses?	You worry for the child all the way through and it doesn't stop even when the parent gets caught because...	

Planning your writing

4   Share what you already know about ways to set out instruction writing, e.g. *use headings, number different...*

5   Your director's notes will give instructions to the rest of the team putting on the production of *Catch*. Use your memory aid **ChASM** and the thinking frame you have just filled in to help you plan.

   a) Work out headings for the different sections of your notes, e.g. *Introduction, Set...*

   b) Decide the order in which you are going to write about the different things.

   c) Decide what you are going to write about under each heading.

 6   Use the thinking frame you completed for question 3 to write the first three paragraphs of your director's notes, where you give an overview of the play. Begin paragraphs on new lines and use the topic sentences you wrote earlier to start them.

   In each section of the director's notes, the instructions given to the cast and stage crew should be in the same order as events happen in the script.

7   Brainstorm the features you expect an instruction text to have and then read the example below and work out:

   a) what number each of the labels is pointing to

   b) where these two extra labels should point:

   i) write in shorter, easy-to-follow sentences   *ii)* use clear, plain language

A Start each new point on a new line, using bullet points, numbers or letters.

C Headings for each section.

Instructions for actor playing the child ¹

It is really important that the audience feels that the parent is being totally unreasonable so:

²● ³start off by making the child ⁴seem just a bit over-tired.

²● ³make the child ⁴appear dreamy and/or silly –
      not deliberately naughty.

B Imperative verbs.

D Present tense.

8   a) As a class write three instructions for lines 1–13 for the actor who is the parent to follow.

   b) In pairs, write more instructions for each actor for lines 14–35.

   c) On your own, write instructions for each actor for lines 36–63.

Thinking about what you have learned

9   Think about what you have done so far and write about how you are doing under these headings:

   I already knew...   *I am learning to...*   *I still need to practise...*

4.4　Writing the director's notes

Objectives:
- *choosing verbs to give instructions*
- *avoiding ambiguity*
- *deciding how formal your tone should be*
- *writing reflectively about* Catch
- *giving specific, easy-to-follow, clearly sequenced directions and instructions.*

Choosing verbs to give instructions

The director's notes include instructions for the actors and production team of *Catch*. Depending on which verb you choose, your instructions can sound forceful, reasonable or more like a suggestion.

1　Rank the list of verb phrases in the box below. Begin with the most forceful and end with those that would make an instruction sound more like a suggestion.

> should　　can　　could　　ought　　insist　　will
> must　　will have to　　demand　　might be a good idea to
> would you mind　　suggest　　require

2　Make a list of other words or phrases you will want to include to sound polite and reasonable, e.g. *perhaps, it would be helpful if...*

3　Work with a friend. Make up a conversation pretending you are new zoo keepers. Each wants to persuade the other to be the first to pick up a scorpion. Use the words and phrases you have been exploring, so that your conversation starts very politely but ends with you ordering each other about.

4　Write an instruction for the actor playing the parent which tells the actor to mime holding a hurt hand, in lines 47–49, so that it:
　a) sounds more like a suggestion
　b) sounds polite and reasonable
　c) sounds more forceful.

Avoiding ambiguity and choosing the right tone

An important part of writing your director's notes is making sure your writing is clear and that it does not sound either too friendly or too formal.

Avoiding ambiguity

You will have to make it very clear which part of the play you are referring to, and who your instructions are for (especially if two actors of the same sex are playing the characters).

5   Read the instructions below and decide:

  a) Four things that make these instructions unclear, e.g. *no numbering... order*

  b) How can you re-write them to make it clear that all the **bold** instructions are meant for the child, and the *italic* ones are meant for the adult?

> **You must look surprised by his reaction.** *You should be furious by now. He should be nearly crying* and **he should look pretty scared at the end**.

6   a) As a class, write very clear instructions for the actors for lines 36–63.

  b) In pairs, check the instructions for actors you have both already written and suggest how each of you can make your instructions clearer.

  c) Re-draft your instructions for each actor so they are as clear as possible.

How formal should the tone of your writing be?

Since you are the director leading the team for whom you are writing the notes it is important that your notes sound as informal and relaxed or as formal and efficient as you want them to be.

7   a) Which of the approaches A, B and C opposite sounds:
  - most formal?
  - least formal?

  Pick out the words or phrases that make them so.

  b) Which tone do you think is best for your piece of writing? Why?

  c) Brainstorm which features you need to use as you write to create the same tone, e.g. *Use 'I' and 'you', or avoid using 'I' and 'you'? Choose common, simple words or...*

8 **a)** As a class, write a paragraph of instructions about how the lighting should change at the end of the play using the same tone as A.

   b) In a group, re-draft the instruction you have just written so that its tone is more like the writing in B.

   c) On your own, write instructions for the lighting crew in the tone that you decided was most appropriate for your instructions.

 9 Now use all that you have learned to write a finished version of the director's notes. Remember to make the instructions clear, say who you are referring to and keep to the right tone.

 Checking instructions

10 Now read and mark a friend's instructions by checking these things:

   a) Are the headings and numbering system helpful and clear?

   b) Tick each instruction that is clear.

   c) Underline any instructions that are not clear and put a note in the margin explaining what you do not understand. How could your friend make them clearer?

   d) Underline any places where the writing becomes less or more formal.

Writing assignment

Major task: you should spend about 40 minutes answering this question.

Your writing will be marked for:

- *how you structure and punctuate sentences (5 marks)*
- *how you organise paragraphs and ensure that the complete piece of writing hangs together (5 marks)*
- *its overall impact on the reader (15 marks)*
- *the accuracy of your spelling (5 marks).*

Setting up instructions

Topline Theatre Group are coming to your school on Monday to perform *Catch* to the whole of Year 7 at 10.00 a.m. Below is a list of things the Theatre Group have asked for. Write a set of instructions telling your school caretaker what has to be set up and arranged so that the visit will go smoothly.

Topline Theatre Group
Catch

High School, Year 7, Monday 4th April, 10 a.m.

To perform **Catch** for your pupils, Topline Theatre Group needs:

- a large room or hall with either a stage or a clear 5 x 5 metre area to act in
- the audience seated in rows on three sides of the acting space
- a screened-off area for actors not on stage, props etc. Ideally this should be behind or to one side of the stage or acting area
- access to main lights
- a parking space for our Luton van so that we can unload props and costumes easily
- the room to ourselves for two hours before and after the performance.

Make a plan using a frame like the one below before you start writing.

When
Who
What things to collect
How they should be arranged
What information to give to Topline Theatre Group when they arrive
Useful words and phrases

This unit helps you explore how writers choose different ways to write about information depending on why they are writing (their purpose) and who their audience is. You will then go on to write two information texts of your own for different audiences.

5.1 Reading non-fiction texts

Objectives:
- *finding the best resources for a task*
- *skimming a text to gain an overview*
- *scanning a text to find information.*

Finding the best resources for a task

1 You have been asked to find out the following information:
   - who invented television?
   - when was it invented?
   - what were the first television programmes like?
   - how does a television set work?

encyclopaedia	dictionary	Internet
thesaurus	a 90-year-old person	

   a) Which of the resources in the box above would be most useful?
   b) Why won't the other resources help?
   c) What other resources would be useful?

2 Explain how you would consult each of the useful resources to find the right information, e.g. *Resource: the Internet. Use a search engine like Google. Then type in...*

Gaining an overview of a text before finding information in it

Being able to find information you need quickly is an important skill. You are going to practise doing this by following these three steps as you study the information in the texts on pages 70–72:

Step 1 *Be clear about why you are reading the text*

- First decide what information you are really looking for.
- Then work out how you will find this information.

3 **a)** What information do you need to find out from this text?
  b) Make a list of the words and phrases a writer uses to write about the sort of information you are looking for – these are the key words you will be skimming the text for, e.g. *'invented by'*, *in [date]…*

Step 2 *Skim the text*

Skim the text to get an overview of what it is about and where different pieces of information are. You can skim through a text by studying the:

- **Headings**
- **Illustrations** – charts, pictures, maps etc.
- **first Paragraph of each section**
- **first Sentence of each paragraph.**

The letters in the word **HIPS** can help you remember this technique.

4 Practise skimming by studying each text in turn and noting what each part is about, e.g. *The first heading… tells you…*

Step 3 *Scan the text*

Scan a text by drawing your forefinger along the text line by line as you let your eyes sweep across it searching for key words. If you see a word that might be about your topic then stop and read that part of the text.

5 **a)** Practise scanning by examining each text and noting as much of the information you need as you can find.
  b) Then list any information you would still like to find out.

Think about what you have learned

6 **a)** What is the difference between skimming and scanning?
  b) Where else could you use the three steps you have practised in this unit?

A

THE Sun

WATCHA

Scientists stunned as 'televisor' beams live pictures on to a screen

By DICKY PICTURE

Inventor John Logie Baird and his ingenious televisor device.

A MAN has invented a miracle gadget called a 'televisor' – out of an old tea chest, some bits of cardboard and string.

It has a postcard-sized screen which shows live, moving images sent from a camera nearby.

Scottish inventor John Logie Baird caused amazement when he demonstrated the contraption yesterday at his flat in London's Soho.

And scientists were last night speculating that homes everywhere might one day have a 'TV' and receive pictures from all over the world.

DUMMY

Baird, 36, has been working on the project for years. He revealed that his big breakthrough came last October when he successfully beamed the image of a ventriloquist's dummy called Stooky Bill on to the screen.

He said: 'The image of the dummy's head formed itself on the screen with what appeared to be an almost unbelievable clarity.

'I had got it! I could scarcely believe my eyes and felt myself shaking with excitement.'

*From **The Sun – Hold ye Front Page** by John Perry and Neil Roberts*

B

Television

¹We watch moving pictures and listen to voices and music on a television set. ²Messages about the pictures and sounds are sent from a transmitter through the air (or along a cable) to your television set.

¹ *direct, personal style*

² *sentences mostly simple or compound*

³ *simpler vocabulary*

How it works

Inside ¹your television is a receiver that reads the ³messages. ²Then the receiver ³tells the screen at the front of the television set how to make the right pictures out of thousands of red, blue and green dots. At the same time the receiver works out what noises the speakers need to make for you to hear the story too.

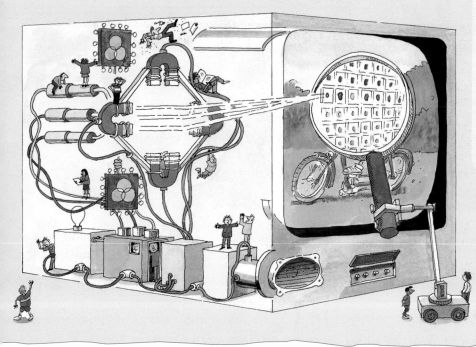

C

Television

As strange as it may seem, all of the action that ¹you see when you watch your favourite show is actually an optical illusion. What appears to be a moving picture is really a series of still pictures that are displayed in rapid ³succession. In fact, 30 different images are flashed across ¹your screen every second. ²As you watch a television programme, your brain merges the pictures together, so the image in front of you seems to move.

¹ *personal style*

² *mixture of sentence types, including ones with subordinate clauses*

³ *more sophisticated vocabulary*

To produce a single one of these pictures, three beams of tiny ³particles known as ³electrons, are fired at the back of the television screen. These beams sweep across the screen from top to bottom, lighting up tiny dots that are either red, green or blue. Your eyes combine these coloured points of light to see an image in full colour.

*From **Everyday Machines** by John Kelly*

D

Moving the beams

The synchronisation decoder must identify the part of the signal that works like a clock to make the electron beams travel across and down the screen at exactly the right speed. In this manner, 30 separate images are flashed across the television screen each and every second.

5.2 Investigating the features of a non-fiction text

Objectives:
- *revising audience and purpose*
- *exploring how writers match the way a text is organised to its purpose*
- *exploring how writers match the language used in a text to its purpose*
- *revising the main features of information and recount texts*
- *using appropriate terminology.*

Revising audience and purpose

As you know, writers suit their texts to the audience who will read it, and tailor their texts so they achieve the purposes for which they are written.

1   Study the way the texts on pages 70–72 are written and illustrated and:

    a) decide which of the audiences below you think each suits best. Why?

       junior (aged 6–8)   **adults**   **teenagers**   **families**

    b) explain how you can tell what the purpose of each text is, e.g.
       Text… is informing… because the picture… and the text…

Recognising how texts are matched to their audience and purpose

 2   As a class, use the thinking frame opposite to help you investigate texts **A** and **C** and decide on the typical features you would expect:

    a) a newspaper recount text to have

    b) an information text to have.

3   Look carefully at the texts on pages 70–72 and decide:

    a) which of the features you listed do all the information texts have

    b) which features can change to suit the audience.

	Newspaper recount	Information text
1 Purpose		
2 Text level How is it laid out on the page? How are ideas organised? In what order is information given?		
3 Sentence level Is it in the first or third person? What is the main verb tense being used? Is it mostly in the active or passive voice? * What is the typical sentence structure and length? How does a writer link sentences, ideas etc.?		
4 Word level What stock words or phrases are used? Is technical or plain vocabulary used?		

* Explanation:

A writer may change some of the standard features of a text type so that it suits its audience better. For example, you might expect an adult newspaper recount to use the passive voice a lot:

e.g. *The first television set **was invented by** John Logie Baird.*

However, if the writer wants a family audience to read it, then using the active voice can make it sound livelier and be more easily understood by younger readers:

e.g. *John Logie Baird invented the first television set.*

4   In groups, find the features in the texts described below and decide why they make each text suit its audience better:

   a) Text **A** is a recount text for families and has single-sentence paragraphs.

   b) Text **B** is an information text for children aged 6–8 and has a cartoon showing little people investigating a television set.

   c) Text **C** is an information text for teenagers and has an informal, chatty style.

   d) Text **D** is an information text for adults and has a sophisticated vocabulary.

5 Work on your own. Which features would you change to make:

   a) Text **C** more suited to an adult audience?

   b) Text **D** more suited to a junior audience?

   c) Text **A** more suited to a teenage audience?

Working out how texts are suited to audience and purpose

6 Copy and complete a flow diagram like the one below showing the steps you need to take to work out how a text suits its audience and purpose:

| 1 Decide who the text is... | → | 2 Decide what... | → | 3 Think about... | → | 4 Investigate... |

5.3 Planning and writing an information text

Objectives:

- *collecting, choosing and planning your ideas*
- *organising a text to suit its content, purpose and audience*
- *selecting and presenting information*
- *drafting a text.*

Collecting and choosing ideas, and planning a text

You are going to write an information text for a pre-teen (9–12) audience about roller-skating.

1 Read this student's notes, then decide:

   a) what other information about roller-skating you could look for that would interest this audience

   b) how you would go about searching for this information.

> 1760 – Invention of roller-skates
>
> By Joseph Merlin – a Belgian musical instrument maker
>
> Merlin wore first pair to a high society event – a masked ball at Carlisle House, Soho, London.
>
> He rolled in to the party wearing his skates and playing the violin but crashed into & smashed a huge ballroom mirror.
>
> 1863 – James Plimpton of New York first patented a 4 wheel version

2   Many pages in information books look a lot like this. Use the rough layout below to help you sketch your page layout, making a note of:

a) what topics you would want to write about

b) where you would place the different sorts of information

c) what sort of illustrations you would want to include.

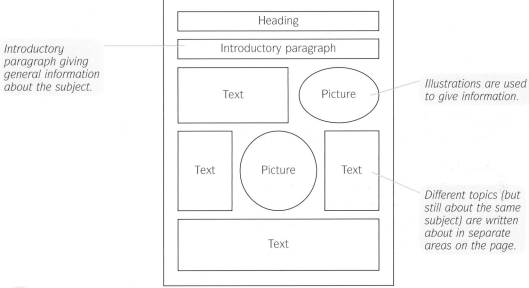

Introductory paragraph giving general information about the subject.

Illustrations are used to give information.

Different topics (but still about the same subject) are written about in separate areas on the page.

 Drafting a text to suit its content, audience and purpose

3   You are only going to write the section about how roller-skates were invented. Think about the reading work you did earlier and decide what features you think an information text for a pre-teen audience should have.

> When you want to write a text for a particular audience it is worth trying out different ways of writing the piece so that you can find the best approach, and if possible trying it out on that audience.

4   Text **B** was written for 6–8 year olds, text **C** for teenagers. Your audience is in between these age groups. Study the labels on **B** and **C** as you compare the way they are written and decide which of these features to use when writing for your pre-teen audience:

a) an impersonal style, e.g. *In 1760 a Belgian musician…*

or b) a personal style, e.g. *You wouldn't believe…*

c) only simple or compound sentences, e.g. *A Belgian called Joseph Merlin invented roller-skates…*

or d) some complex sentences too, e.g. *A Belgian called Joseph Merlin, who was an instrument maker, invented roller-skates…*

e) plain, simple vocabulary, e.g. *cut*

or f) more technical vocabulary, e.g. *lacerated*.

5 This is how one student began their text.

a) What choices has this student made?

b) Write the next two sentences keeping to the same style.

> Did you know that roller-skates were invented nearly 250 years ago? In 1760 Joseph Merlin, who usually made musical instruments, decided to attach some wheels to a pair of boots.

6 Now write your own opening paragraph for your information text in your chosen style.

7 Write several versions of the next paragraph trying out each of the suggestions below, and any ideas of your own, as you explore the best way to make the information about Joseph Merlin's crash memorable.

a) Remind readers of their own crashes while wearing roller-skates, e.g. *Like everyone trying to roller-skate for the first time...*

b) Tell the information more like a story: *Music filled the air and...*

c) Make it humorous.

8 What might you add to your text to make it more helpful, and look more appealing? E.g. *Illustrations of... highlighting these words...*

9 Now read through all the writing you have done and decide which pieces are most effective for:

a) the information you are giving

b) the audience you want to appeal to (you and your friends!)

c) the purpose of the writing.

10 Bear this in mind as you write a final draft of the information text telling readers about Joseph Merlin's invention.

Deciding how to write a text

11 Make a list of five important things you need to think about as you prepare to write an information text. Then decide the order in which you should think about them. E.g.:

1 The style that will suit...

5.4   Writing a recount text for an adult audience

Objectives:
- *writing a recount text for an adult audience*
- *identifying the main point of a paragraph*
- *writing an effective first sentence for your paragraphs*
- *identifying how supporting information relates to the main point.*

Planning a recount text for an adult audience

You are going to write a newspaper story telling of Joseph Merlin's unusual entrance at the 1760 party (on page 74).

 1   Look back at the list of main features of a recount text you made earlier and the example on page 72, and decide how you will make your recount text suit an adult audience.

In a recount text the information can be organised so that:
- **the first paragraph** sums up the main story or news
- **then** readers are told the wider importance of the news
- **lastly** readers are told about the effect of the news on individuals.

2   Study the quotations below, and bearing in mind what you have just read, decide the order in which you will write about these reactions in your recount.

1   *Marguerite Tilley*

It was an extraordinary spectacle – such a dangerous idea. I can't imagine that wheels on boots will ever be popular!

2   *Mr Carp, Carlisle estate manager*

Mr Merlin will be charged for the damage he did to the antique mirror.

What an invention! I can imagine errand boys wanting pairs of boots with wheels too. In fact, I wouldn't mind a pair myself, don't you know!

Next time I will forget the violin.

3   *Lord Toby Nair*

4   *Joseph Merlin*

Writing well-organised paragraphs

Your recount text should have five paragraphs and at the end of it readers should have found out:

Who?   **What?**   **When?**   **Where?**   **Why?**

3   Plan the five paragraphs of your recount in a chart like the one below so that you know what each paragraph will be about and making sure all the quotations from page 77 are included.

Paragraph	Topic
I	Brief summary of what happened...

Although the example of a recount text on page 70 has single-sentence paragraphs, a recount text written for an adult audience can have much more sophisticated paragraphs.

4   Read the paragraph below. Which sentences would you use each of the labels (1–4) to point to?

1   The **topic sentence**.

    The writer goes on to include information which supports the main idea of the paragraph using:

2   A sentence which gives **greater detail**.

3   A sentence which **carries on with the same point**.

4   A sentence which gives **an illustration**, a **quotation** or **proof**. N.B. in a recount a quotation is introduced by a colon and does not have to be set out on a new line.

time connectives to link informatic (see page 106 for others)

impersonal style

After the incident in which Joseph Merlin lost control of his wheeled boots, he needed medical treatment. His cut had to be bandaged and ointment applied. When asked about the accident Joseph Merlin said that there was no problem with his invention but: 'Next time I will forget the violin'. Joseph Merlin's revolutionary new boots with wheels were not damaged by his fall and he intends to wear them in public again.

past tense

sophisticated vocabulary

*Adapted from **The ITN Book of Firsts** by Melvin Harris*

5   As a class, write the second paragraph of the recount beginning with the topic sentence below and telling readers what the boots are like, what they can do, and including one of the quotations on page 77: *The wheeled boots are an extraordinary invention*.

6   On your own, write the third paragraph using what you have learned and beginning: *The invention caused quite a stir amongst...*

 7   Now write a finished version of your recount text so that it is well-organised and each paragraph is packed with detail.

 Writing a recount text with well-organised paragraphs

8   What tips would you give someone about:
   a) planning to write a recount text?
   b) the best way to write well-organised paragraphs?

Reading assignment

This test is 40 minutes long.

- *You should spend the first 5–10 minutes reading the text and questions carefully before you start writing your answers.*
- *Looking at the marks for each question should help you to judge how much to write for each answer.*

The idea that fingerprints could be used to trace criminals came from Charles Darwin's cousin, Francis Galton. He founded the laboratory in which I work at University College London, the first human **genetics** institute in the
5 world. Every day I walk past a collection of relics of his life. They include some rows of seeds that show similarities between parents and offspring, an old copy of *The Times* and a brass counting
10 gadget that can be hidden in the palm of the hand. Each is a reminder of Galton. As well as his revolution in detective work Galton was the first person to publish a weather map and the only one to have
15 made a beauty map of Britain, based on a secret ranking of the local women on a scale of one to five (the low point, incidentally, being in Aberdeen).

His biography reveals an unrelieved **eccentricity**, well illustrated by the
20 titles of a dozen of his three hundred scientific papers: On spectacles for divers; Statistical inquiries into the **efficacy of prayer**; Nuts and men; The average flush of excitement; Visions of sane persons; Pedigree moths; Arithmetic by smell; Three generations of lunatic cats; Strawberry cure for gout; Cutting a round cake on scientific principles; Good and bad temper
25 in English families; *and* The relative sensitivity of men and women at the nape of the neck.

Galton's work led, indirectly, to today's explosion in human genetics. His particular interest was in the inheritance of genius (a class within which he placed himself). In his 1869 book *Hereditary Genius*, he investigated the
30 ancestry of distinguished people and found a tendency for talent to crop up again and again in the same family. This, he suggested, showed that ability was inborn and not acquired. *Hereditary Genius* marked the first attempt to establish patterns of human inheritance with well-defined traits – such as becoming (or failing to become) a judge – rather than with mere **speculation** about vague qualities such as **fecklessness**.

*From **The Language of the Genes** by Professor Steve Jones*

> **genetics** – the study of how we inherit characteristics such as eye or hair colour from our parents
>
> **eccentricity** – odd behaviour
>
> **efficacy of prayer** – whether prayer produces the desired effect
>
> **speculation** – giving opinions without proof
>
> **fecklessness** – being feeble or irresponsible

1   Write down the order you would put the statements below in so each
    topic is in the same order as it appears in the text. (*First, then...*)

    A   Galton wrote a large number of scientific papers.

    B   Galton investigated the idea that humans inherit characteristics.

    C   Francis Galton is still remembered at University College London.

    [1 mark]

2   How do the first sentences of the first and third paragraphs
    help readers understand the information which follows?

    [2 marks]

3   The second paragraph is one long sentence. How does the way
    it is organised help build an impression of Galton's character?

    [2 marks]

4   What do you think Steve Jones was trying to emphasise
    when he included the clause '*he suggested*' in line 31?

    [2 marks]

5   Steve Jones uses brackets three times in the article. These are copied
    below. Look at where they appear in the text, then explain how the
    brackets are being used to make the text, more entertaining to read.

    • (the low point, incidentally, being in Aberdeen) lines 17–18

    • (a class within which he placed himself) lines 28–29

    • (or failing to become) line 34.

    [3 marks]

6   What kind of audience do you think this article is written for?
    Give reasons for your answer.

    [3 marks]

7   Explain how Steve Jones tried to make his information about who
    Francis Galton was, and what he contributed to science, entertaining
    for his audience.
    You must refer to details in the text and to the effect of such features as:

    • the choice of information

    • the vocabulary used

    • the sentence length and structure.

    [16 marks]

In this section you will explore how a journalist wrote a feature article about edible insects for a specific audience, and how the print and images work together. Then you will go on to write a media explanation text for a teenage audience.

6.1 Understanding how writers appeal to their audience

Objectives:
- *identifying how a media text is suited to its audience*
- *discovering how a writer holds readers' attention*
- *investigating vocabulary choices.*

Identifying how a media text is suited to its audience

The writer of the text on pages 84–85 made his writing suit the text's audience and the purpose for which it was written.

1   As you read the text, look out for each of the clues below and decide:
   a) what it suggests about the text's audience and purpose
   b) how it grabs the reader's attention.

Who is the text's audience?

Clue 1

Clue 2   *Ooh, we're jealous!*

Clue 3   *A McCricket burger to go...*

Clue 4   *meg@*   *bugalicious*   *OK*   *(?!)*

What is the text's purpose?

Clue 5   *But why eat these creepy, crawly critters...?*

Clue 6   *they're nutritious, easy to find...*

Clue 7   *termites are collected in a bowl of water...*

Discovering how a writer holds readers' attention

All writers need to hold their readers' attention. They may try to amuse, intrigue, surprise, amaze or puzzle you. They want to engage your interest and possibly arouse some emotions about, or reactions to, what they are saying.

2   Brainstorm a list of ways a writer can try to do this, e.g. *amuse readers by using puns, wordplay or... surprise readers by suggesting something strange is a good idea... intrigue you by...*

   Now find out which of your ideas the writer of the text on pages 84–85 used, and whether they used any techniques you have not suggested.

 3   Copy and complete a table like the one below. Re-read down to line 31 thinking carefully about the way the text is written as you examine each highlighted section and explain:

   a) what effect it will have on its teenage reader.

   b) why it will have this effect. To work this out you need to look closely at the exact words the writer chose and whether the writer used:

   alliteration   onomatopoeia   metaphor   simile

   (remind yourself of the meaning of each of these words by searching for their definitions on the chart on pages 36–37)

   or whether it was phrased as a:

   question   exclamation   command   boast

Example	*Effect on teenage reader*	*Why it has this effect*
'Sizzling scorpions'	entertains	The repeated 's' sound echoes the idea of 'sizzling' and teases the reader. This alliteration reminds them of delicious fried food but then it is being used about scorpions which the reader is not sure about eating!

1 —— *

BUGGIN' YOU

2 —— *
Sizzling scorpions, fried ants and roast witchety-grubs... with these insects you are really spoiling us!

3 —— *
Of the five million insects known to man, a juicy 1,462 are edible. But why eat these creepy, crawly critters which, like mosquitoes, usually
5 sink their teeth into us? Well, with about a billion insects to every man, there's no shortage of cookable critters. And they're nutritious, easy to find, they make a lot less mess than a cow
10 and, apparently, they're very tasty. Bug-gobbling is common in over 100 countries – including Britain. *meg@* discovered what's on the menu where. Go on, tickle your tastebuds!

4 —— *
Africa

5 —— *
ON THE MENU: ROASTED TERMITES
                        SALTED WORMS

15 Termites are the world's most popular insects – after grasshoppers – and, in Uganda, they're fried before the heads are removed and the bodies seasoned to perfection with salt. Irresistible! The
20 termites are collected in a bowl of water, cunningly placed under a light – they're attracted to the beam and fall in the water. Anyone can tuck into the winged specimens, but queens are reserved for
25 adults. Ooh, we're jealous! Mopane worms are so popular in southern Africa that experts are devising ways to farm them to avoid extinction. The slippery sliders can't be salted and dried until
30 their bright green and yellow juicy insides are squeezed out. Yikes!

South America

ON THE MENU: CANNED GRASSHOPPERS
                        ROASTED ANTS
                        BAKED TARANTULA

Fresh or preserved grasshopper for you, sir? In Mexico the hopsters are available either way, but always cooked, so the

35 colour changes from a grey/brown to a more appetising (?!) red. Colombians prefer filling up on ants. If you're ever offered a slice of toast spread with a thick layer of brown sludge, don't assume it's 40 Marmite; its more likely to be ground-up ants. You can also buy bucketfuls of roast crawlers when you visit the cinema. Just don't throw them at the people in front! Arachnophobics should avoid Venezuela 45 where fire-roasted *Theraphosa leblondi* (that's the world's largest tarantula) has long been pukker tukker for the Yanomani Indians. Once cooked, the white meat inside the legs and abdomen tastes like 50 smoked crab and, since the *Theraphosa* is bigger than an outstretched hand, there's plenty to go round!

USA

ON THE MENU: INSECT SPAGHETTI
CRISPY CRICKETS

'A McCricket burger to go please, and hold the mayo!' OK, so you won't hear 55 this just yet, but bugalicious dishes are taking off in America. Sweet company HotLix sells its candy-coated scorpions

and Cricket Lick-It lollies by the thousand. Bug-eaters in the deep south still indulge 60 in a New Year's Day feast of Hoppin' Jons: deep-fried crickets with rice and peas. The US authorities are also more tolerant when it comes to creepies crawling into food: up to 225 insect fragments are 65 allowed in 100g of spaghetti and 60 bug bums in 100g chocolate. Food for thought!

B

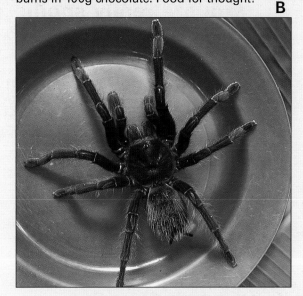

If you're brave enough, you can tuck into some ticklers at Tellington Museum where **Eating Creepy Crawlies** is now on!

From meg@ section of **The Times**, *5 August 2000*

4 As you read lines 32–66 make a similar table to the one on page 83 and this time:

   a) choose eight more words and phrases that will make readers react. Search for words that are dramatic, surprising or very descriptive, or choose questions, exclamations, boasts etc.

   b) explain **what effect** the words and phrases you choose will have on a teenage reader.

   c) explain **why** each of them will have this effect.

Reading for a reaction

5 Make a chart explaining and giving examples of the different techniques writers can use to grab readers' attention and look out for them when you are reading newspaper or magazine articles.

6.2 Examining the impact of words and pictures

Objectives:
- *investigating how joining words together can change their meaning*
- *investigating how suffixes and prefixes affect a word's meaning*
- *recognising how print and pictures work together.*

Investigating how the meaning of words can be changed

Some of the most striking words in the article *Buggin' You* are made by the writer joining two words together.
- Such words may be **compounds**,
  e.g. *taste + buds   out + stretched   colour + blind   tea + pot,*
- or two words blended together, e.g. *giant + enormous = ginormous*

When you want to work out what a made-up word means think about:
- what the combined words mean when they are unjoined or unblended
- what job the word is doing in its sentence, e.g. *describing an object*.

1 **a)** Work out how each of the following words were made, and what they mean:
   - bug-gobbling (line 11)
   - hopsters (line 33)
   - McCricket (line 53)
   - bugalicious (line 55).

   b) Why will these words appeal to teenagers more than to adults?

2 How many 'bug' or insect words can you make in **two minutes** (either by blending two words together or making a compound)? *Bugtastic!*

More common words can be made up of different parts too. Understanding what the different parts mean can help you work out a word's meaning:

prefix	stem	suffix
dis	cover	ed

3 Use the table opposite to help you explain how changing the prefix or suffix has altered the meaning of these phrases in the text, e.g. *In line... it meant... now it means...*
   - '1,462 insects are **in**edible...' (line 2)
   - '**un**usually sink their teeth...' (lines 4–5)
   - 'they're **mal**nutritious' (line 8)
   - 'they're very taste**less**...' (line 10)

Prefix	ex	in/un	mal	re
means	former	not/the opposite	bad	again/back
Suffix	**able**	**ed**	**ful**	**less**
means	able/worthy	shows it is in the past	full of	without

Recognising how print and pictures work together

When you look at a text you 'read' pictures, colours and visual elements before you read any words. Asking yourself these six questions can help you better understand what the picture is saying:

Questions to ask	Answers responding to picture A
1 **What is the main idea?**	A girl happily biting a spider kebab.
2 **What ideas are suggested by the way the people and animals are shown?**	Usually we think of spiders biting or eating humans but this time it's the other way round – surprisingly the girl is eating the spider.
3 **Where is it?**	Towards the centre, so that the page layout is balanced and therefore more attractive.
4 **How big is it?**	Larger than any other and takes up about a third of the space so it grabs your attention, which gives its idea greater impact.
5 **What style is it? (photograph, cartoon etc.)**	This is a photograph, so the reader knows that a real girl really is eating those insects.
6 **How is a reader likely to react to it?**	That's horrible! How can she?

4 Now look at picture **B**. Answer the same questions about it and note down what the photograph adds to the article.

> You can also use similar questions when you want to think about what impact
> - different types of headings
> - print
> - colours
>
> have in a text. As you do this, remember that writers choose each picture, type of print and colour to make the text appealing and to strengthen the ideas being expressed in the words in the text.

5 Look at the label lines (1–5) pointing to different features of the media text on page 84. Explain:
   a) what each feature is
   b) what impact it has.

6   How has the choice of pictures **A** and **B** helped to strengthen the sort of reaction readers will have when they read the opening of *Buggin' You*?

Understanding media texts

7   Tell a friend six things you have discovered that can help a media text have impact.

6.3   Writing a media explanation text

Objectives:
- *planning an explanation text so that it appeals to its audience*
- *selecting information to suit a text's audience and purpose*
- *revising the features of explanation texts*
- *investigating different ways of organising paragraphs*
- *expanding your choice of link words and phrases.*

Planning an explanation text to suit a particular audience

1   Discuss how the writer of the *Buggin' You* article on pages 84–85 made sure it suited its teenage audience, and make a list of techniques that you can use in your own writing, e.g. *Chatty, friendly style... some slang, trendy words, humour... knows a teenage audience will feel... about eating insects so...*

Work in a group. *meg@* have asked your team to write an article for teenage readers explaining different activities that teenagers can try out in your area during the summer holidays.

2   Use a thinking frame like the one below and brainstorm all the suitable activities your group knows enough about to write an article.

Activities for teenagers	in dry weather	in wet weather
Things to do at home		
Places you can go to		

 3   Make sure each person in the group will be able to write about a different activity. Then copy and complete the double page spread design opposite to help you work out the best way of laying out the different parts of your article. Include:

Heading   **Introduction**   **Different sections**   **2 pictures**

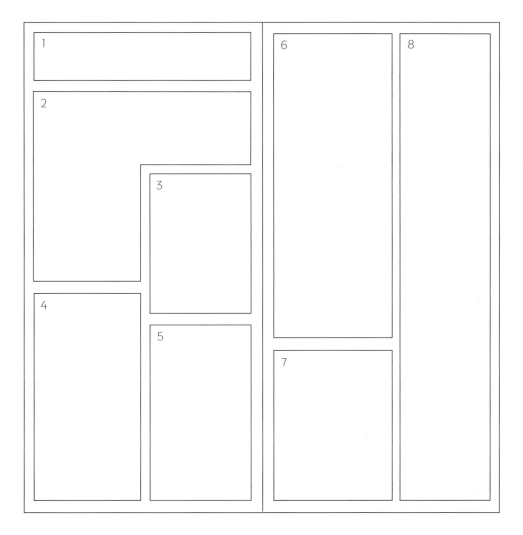

4 **a)** Use the spider diagram below to help you think about the different
      sorts of information you should include in your article.
   b) Then make a plan showing what you will put in each paragraph of
      the part of the article you are writing.

Organising paragraphs in an explanation text

5 As a class, discuss the features you expect an explanation text to have using the *Buggin' You* article to help you. E.g. *Start with... present tense...*

6 Read the explanations and examples below that describe three different ways writers can organise information in paragaraphs. Then decide which method is being used in *Buggin' You* in:
   a) lines 15–31
   b) lines 32–52.

> **You can organise information in a paragraph by writing:**
>
> • in the same order as events happen, e.g. **First** *book a court at Headley Leisure Centre which has...* **Then** *make sure you...* **Finally** *take...*
> • in order of importance, e.g. **The most important fact** *to remember is that* **if** *you keep your eyes on the ball* **then**... **Make sure you** *also...*
> • so that different pieces of information are compared, e.g. *In Cheam it is (like this)... In Acton it is (different).* **On the one hand**... **on the other hand**...

7 Make a list of connectives that you will be able to use to link sentences when you use each method of organising information.

8 a) Which method of organising information would be the best to use when you write the first paragraph, where you are explaining to the reader what information is included in the article?
   b) As a group write a first draft of the first paragraph of your article making sure (a) it begins with a topic sentence, (b) it is well organised, and (c) it contains the most appropriate link words.

9 Now work on your own as you think about the part of the article you are writing. Look at your plan and decide:
   a) which method of organising the information in a paragraph you will use in each of your paragraphs
   b) which connectives you will need to use to do that.

10 Write your part of the article making sure the way you write really suits your audience, and that your paragraphs begin with topic sentences. Organise the other sentences in the best way.

Comparing texts

11 Compare pieces of writing with the rest of your group and discuss whether:
   a) each paragraph is easy to read and follow
   b) one of the other methods of organising the information would work better. If so, why?

6.4 Giving informal advice

Objectives:
- *reviewing handwriting*
- *using presentational devices*
- *giving informal advice*
- *organising information*
- *expanding your choice of link words and phrases.*

Reviewing your handwriting and presentation ⓦⓢ

1 Brainstorm a list of features that make handwriting easy to read.

2 Look at the advice below and suggest five ways this writer can improve her handwriting.

> When your family comes to Sissencester these are the best places to visit. Waterworld Theme Park. You can try waterski-ing, jet ski-ing water polo, swimming, It's A Knockout games and lots more. ~~Their~~ There are things to suit every age.
>
> The Living Museum is also worth a visit. It has enormous models of human organs that you can walk through , animals to see, film clips and lots of information...

3 Where could this writer have used:
   a) headings
   b) underlined words
   c) bullets
   d) a numbered list to make the information in this text easier for the reader to follow?

4   Now look at a recent piece of non-fiction you have written. Compare it with the writing in the example on page 91 and make a list of things you need to do to improve your handwriting and presentation.

5   How can you set out your writing in other subjects (for instance Geography or History) using headings, bullets and spacing to present it better?

> When you are writing during this unit try to carry out the changes you know are needed to improve your handwriting and presentation.

Giving informal advice

The editor of *meg@* wants you to include a section in your article which gives informal advice to teenage wheelchair users about:

- which leisure activities your group has suggested that will suit them
- whether there are other activities they can find out about which are local and might also suit them.

6   Discuss what information you could include in this section that will suit this audience's needs, and will interest them. Decide how many paragraphs you will write and which of the methods of organising paragraphs you examined on page 90 you will use to organise them.

7   Look at the way the advice below was written. Use it to:
   a) help you brainstorm the features that a piece of writing giving informal advice should have, e.g. *an opening sentence that... The writer writes in the... tense and uses verbs like... Sentences are... The tone is ...*
   b) make a list of link words or phrases, and any other vocabulary in the example below that you can use in your own piece of writing. Add more suggestions to this list, e.g. *perhaps you could... you might wish to... another option is... some people prefer...*

> *Have you ever considered visiting Ripley Park? There are plenty of attractions to suit the whole family:*
> - *your young children will enjoy the pet zoo where they can touch and feel the animals*
> - *adults can try...*

8   The example above was written for adults and is quite formal and serious in tone. What changes might you make so that your writing suits your teenage audience? E.g. *Sound more relaxed and chatty. Include...*

9   The student below has begun a paragraph describing the local leisure
    centre. Complete the paragraph advising the reader that:
    a) the lift is too narrow for a wheelchair
    b) there is a stair lift and helpers are available from 10 a.m.–6 p.m.
    c) The café, badminton and volleyball courts are upstairs.

> There is good wheelchair access to the ground floor of
> Sissencester Leisure Centre. This means that you can make
> use of the swimming pool and the gym. There are special
> changing rooms and toilets for disabled people. Unfortunately...

10 Use what you have learned as you write the advice section for your article.

Getting ready to give advice

11 How would you reply to this letter sent to an agony aunt?

Dear Experienced Writer,

I've been offered an agony column in *meg@* but I
don't know how to write down the advice that
people are asking for. What advice can you give me?

Yours,

Ivor Worry

Writing assignment

Major task: you should spend about 40 minutes answering this question.

Your writing will be marked for:
- *how you structure and punctuate sentences (5 marks)*
- *how you organise paragraphs and ensure that the complete piece of writing hangs together (5 marks)*
- *the overall impact of your writing on the reader (15 marks)*
- *the accuracy of your spelling (5 marks).*

A magazine for parents wants you to write an article about award-winning chef and TV personality Rainsly Herriot's new restaurant 'Bugalicious'.

Use the information opposite as you write for **parents** to:
- **explain** how popular eating insects is
- **explain** how different insects are prepared and cooked at the restaurant
- **explain** what different insects taste like
- **advise** which insects to try for their first meal.

Plan your writing carefully

Think carefully about what presentation features you will use in your writing, e.g. *headings, numbering, bullet points etc.*

Your page can include two pictures. Do not draw them. Instead:
- leave a space for each
- explain briefly what each would show
- write the caption.

What's on offer at Bugalicious

African roasted or fried termites — taste like nuts

African Mopane worms are salted and dried after their green and yellow insides are squeezed out. Taste like crisps

*Locusts — scattered over pizza or pasta

*Mexican canned grasshoppers — grey/brown — with pasta or rice

Stink bugs — taste like apples

*Dragonflies taste fishy — can be boiled, or candy-coated for dessert

Canned baby bees — a Japanese delicacy

Witchety grubs — taste of scrambled eggs and mozzarella

Colombian roasted ants spread on toast — taste like nuts

Venezuelan baked tarantula — tastes like smoked crab
American deep fried crickets — taste tangy — served with rice and peas

American chocolate-coated scorpions

*Aborigine Bogong moth cake

Australian raw honeypot ants — sweet

Insects are high in protein low in fat.

*These are on the three-course set menu costing £12.00

This unit helps you practise investigating evidence as you decide whether each of the people mentioned in the texts on page 102 were victims of spontaneous human combustion. When you have reached a conclusion you will write a fair and balanced discussion of the evidence.

7.1 Studying evidence

Objectives:
- *distinguishing between fact and opinion*
- *finding relevant information in texts*
- *deciding whether the information is valid and reliable.*

Investigating evidence

When you are investigating evidence you need to look beyond how strongly someone believes in what they are saying and think carefully about the quality of the information they give you. Following these two steps will help you do this:
- *First, decide what is* **fact** *and what is* **opinion***.*
- *Then, ask yourself if the information is:*
  relevant   **valid**   **reliable**

Distinguishing between fact and opinion

1   Explain the difference between a fact and an opinion.

2   Divide into groups to play **Auction**.

  i)   Each group chooses a different object in the room such as a *chair* or *radiator*.

  ii) Members of the group jot down at least 5 facts which are true and 5 opinions about their object (some of the opinions can be outrageous, e.g. *possibly the finest example of Victorian carpentry in our school!*).

  iii) Choosing one member of their group to be the auctioneer, the groups take it in turns to auction their object, using all the facts and opinions, e.g. *What am I bid for this sturdy, brown chair? Possibly the only example...*

  iv) As the other groups listen to the sales speech they note down as many of the facts and opinions as they can. Then each group counts up their score (3 facts and 2 opinions = 5) and bids with it.

  v)   The first group able to offer the auctioneer the highest bid of facts and opinions (and be able to explain which is which) 'buys' the object.

Evaluating material

Now you are ready to search for evidence that will help you discuss the question:

Were each of the dead people mentioned in the texts on page 102 victims of spontaneous human combustion?

> **Making sure information is relevant**
>
> Information can only be used as evidence for your discussion if it is relevant. To work out what information is relevant to the question:
>
> - Pick out the most important words and phrases in the question you are investigating, e.g. '*each* of the *dead people*'.
> - Decide what sort of information you need to find to be able to answer your question, e.g. Look at what happened to each person separately...
> - Then make sure you scan for this **relevant** information and ignore information that does not help answer the question.

3   What are the key ideas in the question you are discussing in this unit?

4   What sort of information do you need to look for in order to answer the question? E.g. *How each person died... what spontaneous human combustion is...*

> **Making sure information is valid and reliable**
>
> As you study the relevant information:
>
> - decide what is fact and what is opinion. Remember fact is more trustworthy than opinion.
> - look at who is giving the information and where it came from. Facts or opinions given by an expert in a relevant field, e.g *a forensic scientist*, are likely to be more reliable than opinions from someone who is not an expert in any relevant field, e.g. *a bus driver*.
> - compare sources of information to find information that is agreed on.

5   Which of these sources would you expect to give the most valid and reliable information and which the least? Put them in rank order.

> detective   uninvolved scientist
> someone who believes in spontaneous human combustion
> witness   experienced worker

6 As you examine **A–J** on pages 102-103 note each piece of information that is relevant to your investigation and decide how reliable and valid it is by using a checking chart like the one below.

Information	Source	Reliable?	Fact/ opinion	Reason?
a) Jack Larber's clothing caught fire	B - newspaper article	Maybe	Fact	journalists are supposed to be accurate
b) Jack was alone in the hospital room		Yes	Fact	in text E his nurse agrees with facts (b) and (c)
c) Jack was a non-smoker			Fact	

Investigating evidence

7 What advice about how to judge different people's evidence would you give to someone investigating a mystery?

7.2 Examining points of view and reaching a conclusion

Objectives:
- *investigating the way a writer expresses a view*
- *distinguishing between the writer's point of view and that of other people quoted in the text*
- *considering all the information and reaching a conclusion.*

Investigating how a writer expresses a point of view

1 a) Read text **K** opposite. It describes how hard it is to completely burn a human body. As you read, pick out words and phrases that emphasise:
- that this is the speaker's point of view
- the reliability of that view
- the strength of that view.

b) Try to explain why the words you chose for each group are effective.

c) Brainstorm more words and phrases to add to each group of words.

K *'In my experience it is not easy to burn the human body,'* Cremationist Sam Fern explained. *'In fact when a body is cremated it takes 3–4 hours of temperatures in excess of 1,500 degrees. Even then, there are always skeletal remains left over that have to be ground down to ash before the remains can be placed in an urn. I believe it is impossible to reduce a body to complete ash using just fire. In my opinion something mysterious would have to accompany the fire for a body to be totally destroyed.'*

Source: **Cremationist's Weekly**

2 Do you agree that Sam Fern believes it is easy to completely burn the human body? Write your point of view making sure your choice of words emphasises that your view is both strongly held and reliable, e.g.
I am convinced that... it is beyond question... there can be no doubt...

Recognising how writers show they disagree with a view

3 In text **L** below two writers discuss another writer's ideas about Mary Reeser's death. As you read the text, decide what information is relevant and valid for your investigation into how Mary Reeser died.

L *'Nor,'* adds Arnold (who is **only a bus driver**), *'did the carpet beyond her incinerated chair show signs of damage.'*

In fact, the walls and the floors of Mrs Reeser's apartment were of concrete. When last seen by her physician son, Mrs Reeser had been sitting in the big chair, wearing inflammable nightclothes, and smoking cigarette after cigarette – after having taken two Seconal sleeping pills and stating her intention of taking two more. The official police report concluded:

'Once the body became ignited, almost complete destruction occurred from the burning of its own fatty tissues.' (Mrs Reeser was a 'plump' woman, and a quantity of 'grease' – obviously fatty residue from her body – was left at the spot where the immolation occurred.) As the fat liquefied in the fire, it could have been absorbed into the chair stuffing to fuel still more fire to attack still more of the body.

In his relentless drive to foster any sort of mystery, in this and other cases, Arnold raises many questions. For example he wonders why a victim's leg or nearby combustibles are not burned. The answer is that fire tends to burn upward; it burns sideways with some difficulty. Anyone with camping experience has seen a log that was laid across a campfire reduced to ashes by the following morning while the butt ends of the log remained intact.

Source: **Dr Joe Nickell**, private investigator, and **Dr John Fisher**, forensic analyst in the Sheriff's crime laboratory, Orange County, Orlando

4 Now examine the text and list different ways the writers, Dr Joe Nickell and Dr John Fisher try to convince readers that their point of view is right and that Larry Arnold's is wrong. (Three are already in bold.) E.g. *They call Arnold 'only' a bus driver because they are learned experts and he...*

5 Re-consider all the information you gathered from texts A–J. Is it all still as reliable and valid or has any of this new information from texts K and L changed its value?

6 Follow the steps below to decide whether any, or all, of the people in the texts could have been victims of spontaneous human combustion.

a) First draw up a chart like the one below:

Reasons for deciding whether each of the dead people mentioned in the texts on page 102 were victims of spontaneous combustion.	
For	**Against**
Jack Larber was a non-smoker	Maybelle Andrews' dress could have touched someone's lit cigarette butt as she was outside

b) Under **For**, list all your reasons for believing any or each person was a victim of spontaneous human combustion, e.g. *Jack Larber was a non-smoker...*

c) Under **Against**, list your reasons for doubting that any or all those people were victims of spontaneous human combustion, e.g. *Maybelle Andrews' dress could have touched someone's lit cigarette butt as she was outside...*

d) Finally, weigh up the reasons in the two lists and work out your overall conclusion. You might decide that all, some or none of the people were victims of spontaneous human combustion.

 Thinking about the techniques you have used

7 Make a flow chart beginning like the one below showing how you should go about thinking through an issue.

START: Work out what the key words in the issue are...	→		→	

7.3 Planning a discussion text

Objectives:
- *signalling the stages in your argument*
- *planning a discussion text*
- *using a range of evidence to validate your argument*
- *highlighting cause and effect by drawing conclusions*
- *presenting findings fairly*
- *developing well-organised paragraphs.*

You will need to use the information and ideas you have already gathered as you write a discussion of this question for an adult audience:

Were Mary Reeser, Maybelle Andrews and Jack Larber all victims of spontaneous human combustion?

Signalling the stages in your argument

As you write your discussion each paragraph will need to carry a different part of the argument. To help readers know where the discussion is going next, writers use words and phrases like those in the box below.

1   Sort these words and phrases into those you can use to show you are:
    a) adding another idea that agrees with the last
    b) about to give a different view
    c) going to write a paragraph that gives a balanced argument.

> On the one hand   On the other hand   Again
> And another point is   Instead it could be   Moreover
> In the same way   Still   Yet   Nevertheless
> An alternative way of explaining this   However   Furthermore
> In addition   Besides   In conclusion   To sum up

2   Choose one phrase from each group to help you plan a three-point discussion of each of these topics:

On the one hand... Furthermore... However...

A   School uniform should be abolished.
B   Students should be paid for schoolwork.
C   No one should be allowed to smoke.

Spontaneous Human Combustion – fact or fiction?

A **spontaneous human combustion** (SHC) is said to occur when a living human being catches fire without the application of heat from an external source.

B Jack Larber *January 31st*

Jack Larber, who was a 72-year-old patient at the Laguna Honda Home in San Francisco, had his clothing catch fire a few minutes after being fed. His attendant was out of the room at the time it happened but attempted to put out the fire when returning back into the room. Mr Larber died of third-degree burns on February 2nd. No explanation was found for the fire. Mr Larber was a non-smoker.

Source: website on Spontaneous Human Combustion

C Mary Reeser *July 2nd*

The remains of a 67-year-old widow named Mary Reeser were found by her neighbour and some house painters. She had been sitting in an easy chair when the incident happened. Her left foot still wearing a slipper remained intact and only the corner of the room and the chair she was sitting in had been burnt. Firemen, police and pathologists examined Mrs Reeser's remains and also found her liver, which was fused to a lump of vertebrae, and her skull, which had been shrunk to the size of a baseball by the unusually intense heat. The walls of the apartment were covered with a greasy substance, plastic switches had melted along with two candles although the wicks had been left unburnt. There was only a small circular burn area which encompassed the remains of Mrs Reeser and her chair.

Source: website

D Maybelle Andrews *October*

Maybelle Andrews and her boyfriend were leaving a nightclub which did not allow smoking in the main hall (but smoking was allowed just outside the main hall and elsewhere in the building).

Suddenly flames erupted at the hem of Maybelle's dress and spread quickly. Her boyfriend was severely burned trying to put the flames out. He said there were no other flames in the room anywhere and that they had come out of Maybelle herself. Maybelle died on the way to the hospital.

Source: notebook of journalist Ted Bagg, Daily Chronicle

E

'I couldn't believe it – when I left him the guy was sitting up eating his lunch. A few minutes later when I get back he's a mass of flames. That just can't happen. It's not even like he smoked or anything.'

Source: Jack Larber's nurse

G

The idea that the body can burn like a candle isn't so far-fetched at all. In a way, a body is like a candle inside out. With a candle the wick is on the inside, and the fat on the outside. As the wick burns the candle becomes molten and the liquid is drawn onto the wick and burns. With a body, which consists of a large amount of fat, the fat melts and is drawn onto the clothing which acts as a wick, and then continues to burn.

Source: Dr Dougal Drysdale, Edinburgh University

F

Except for a slippered foot, Mrs Reeser's body was largely destroyed, along with the overstuffed chair in which she had been sitting and an adjacent end table and lamp (except for the latter's metal core). The rest of the apartment suffered little damage. Nor did the carpet beyond her incinerated chair show signs of fire damage.

*Source: Larry Arnold, a Pennsylvanian school bus driver and author of **Ablaze**, a book which argues that SHC does occur*

H

Smouldering heat can consume entire pieces of furniture without fire breaking out.

Source: Fire scene forensic investigator

I

There are two reasons why I think the Candle Effect theory is flawed:

1. It has never been successfully reproduced under laboratory conditions.

2. It requires so many hours of burning to go unnoticed.

Source: Prof Edward Storey

J

The foot of Dr John Irving Bentley was all that remained following his death by spontaneous human combustion, 5 December 1966, Northern Pennsylvania, USA.

Planning discursive writing and organising paragraphs

3 Brainstorm what you already know about the features of discursive writing. Then use text **K** to add to your ideas, e.g. *An introduction telling readers... ...tense linking words such as...*

4 **a)** How can you make sure your discussion is fair?
b) Why is it important to be fair when you are writing a discussion? *Hint: think about what your **readers** expect and need.*

WS 5 Start planning your discussion of the question (printed **in bold** on page 101). The chart you made on page 100 will be useful here.
a) List three things you should put in your introduction, e.g *an explanation of what spontaneous human combustion is...*
b) Then work out:
- how many paragraphs you will have in each section of your discussion
- what the main point of each paragraph will be, e.g. *paragraph 4: comparing the evidence about Jack Larber's death in B and E*
- which of the phrases or words you investigated on page 101 you might want to begin each paragraph with.

6 As you read the points below about paragraphs in discursive writing, list four features you will need to include in your own writing.

*The main idea of the paragraph is summed up in the **topic sentence**. It begins with a phrase which signals to the reader which direction the discussion is taking.*

Moreover, witnesses said they could not see how Maybelle and Jack caught fire.

Maybelle's boyfriend's statement says: 'there were no flames in the room' therefore Maybelle could not have been set alight by someone's lighter.

Similarly the report on Jack says he was in hospital and a non-smoker so he would not have had matches or a lighter.

The writer can draw reasonable conclusions from the evidence (red words).

Furthermore patients are not even allowed cigarettes, lighters or matches in their rooms in hospital so it is not very likely there would have been any in his room either...

The writer goes on to include information which supports the main idea of the paragraph using sentences which:

*a) give **an illustration** or **quotation***

*b) **carry on with the same point** offering more **proof***

*c) give **greater detail** while arguing the point*

7   Now look at the evidence you have grouped together in your plan
    to support your points.

    a) How many different sorts of evidence are you offering?

    b) Work out how and where you can add more types of evidence,
        e.g *by counting the number of victims who did not smoke...*

8   The student below has begun a paragraph discussing the death of
    Maybelle. Finish this paragraph taking care to organise the different
    pieces of information you discuss carefully.

> However, it is unlikely that one of the women was a victim
> of spontaneous human combustion. Although the hall where
> she had been dancing was a non-smoking area, Maybelle was
> outside it when she caught fire. In fact, she was in an
> area where...

9   Now write your introduction paragraph and two others taking care to
    signal to the reader where the argument is going, and organising your
    evidence and discussion in each paragraph carefully.

Planning discussions

What are the main things to remember about how to organise reasons
for agreeing or disagreeing when you are planning a discussion text?

7.4   Editing and drafting a discussion

Objectives:

- *expanding the range of link words you use in your sentences*
- *writing a discursive text*
- *using standard English*
- *presenting your findings.*

Expanding your range of link words

In discursive writing you need to link ideas and sentences together so that
the connection between your ideas is clear to your reader. Choosing the
right connective helps you do this.

1 Which connective is used to contrast the different ideas in this sentence?

   Arnold believes Mary Reeser's death was caused by spontaneous human combustion; however, Dr Nickell argues her lit cigarette was to blame.

2 The connectives in the box below can be used to show how one idea follows on from, or contradicts, another idea. Read and sort them into three groups by asking yourself:
   a) which ones do I already know and use?
   b) which ones do I know but do not use?
   c) which ones are new to me? Then think about what the ones in this group mean and how you could use them.

therefore	thus	hence	so	since
which suggests that		because	furthermore	
however	which means that		despite this	
which leads to	moreover			

3 Practise using these connectives by working in teams to play this game.
   i) Your teacher starts by making a statement about the mystery, e.g. *Mary Reeser had taken two sleeping pills*.
   ii) Teams compete to see who can be the first to link another clause on to the teacher's using a logical connective and so score a point, e.g. ***therefore*** *she might not have noticed the fire starting*.
   iii) Continue playing, adding ideas and sentences. The game ends when all the connectives have been used.

 Writing a discussion text ⓦⓢ

4 Read the paragaraph below and decide how the writer could have linked the ideas together better.

   Remember only Mary Reeser were a smoker, none of the rest of them victims could've been set light to. The candle theory sounds dead impressive but just how convincing is it? I think it is poor science because you can't make it happen in a laboratory under perfect conditions, never mind in someone's lounge and impossible in a few minutes in a nightclub! The only answer is that Mary Reeser may've been killed by spontaneous human combustion, Maybelle Andrews and Jack Larber definitely were.

Using standard English

When writers want their discussion to be taken seriously they give it more weight by writing in a formal way using standard English.

5   **a)** Which words or phrases in the passage you have just read are non-standard English? E.g. *Mary Reeser **were** a smoker...*

   b) Which words or phrases make it sound informal? E.g. *could've*.

6   Re-draft the paragraph by changing it to formal, standard English.

7   Write the rest of your discussion, **but not your conclusion**, using all that you have learned and making sure you write in formal, standard English.

Reaching a conclusion

In the final paragraph your discussion should:
- give your final conclusion
- sum up the evidence that made you reach that conclusion.

8   Re-read the text on the previous page and decide where:
   a) the final conclusion is given
   b) the writer summed up the evidence.

9   Which words or phrases made the conclusion quite persuasive?

10   The writer below has still given a personal opinion but without trying to write as persuasively. Compare the two conclusions.
   a) Which sounds
      - more serious?
      - more trustworthy?
   b) Which sort of writing is better in a formal discussion? Why?

> *I believe that the three people were not all victims of spontaneous human combustion. Jack Larber is most likely to have been a victim since he was the only non-smoker, and being cared for in a hospital where...*

11   Complete the paragraph above making sure you also sum up how Mary Reeser and Maybelle may have caught fire. Sound serious and trustworthy.

12   Write the conclusion of your own discussion in the most suitable style.

Writing discussion texts

Listen to each other's conclusions and choose the most effective one.
Then make a copy of it and add labels pointing to its most important features.

Writing assignment

Minor task: you should spend about 25 minutes answering this question.

Your writing will be marked for:
- *your choice and use of vocabulary (4 marks)*
- *how you structure and punctuate sentences and organise paragraphs (4 marks)*
- *the overall impact of your writing on the reader (12 marks).*

You are going to write a discussion of the question:

Should mobile phones be banned in your school?

You can use these ideas and others of your own in your discussion:

> They are a nuisance when they go off in lessons.

> If you have to stay late you can always phone your mum.

> Texting is ruining students' ability to write good English.

1 Before you start writing make some brief notes in a planning frame like the one below to help organise your ideas:

	Main point	*Support this with...*
Introduction		
Arguments for		
Arguments against		
Conclusion		
Linking words or phrases		

A8 Comparing campaigns

This unit will help you understand how writers craft persuasive leaflet and website campaign texts before you write your own charity campaign text.

8.1 Understanding how campaigns are presented

Objectives:
- *identifying the main ideas and points in a text*
- *practising skimming skills*
- *understanding how ideas are sequenced and developed*
- *exploring how writers prepare their readers for a text's ending.*

Identifying the main ideas in a text

1   Revise how to **skim** a text. Check your ideas against the advice on page 69 then skim the text on page 113 quickly so that you can explain:
    a) what it is about
    b) who its audience is
    c) what its purpose is.

2   As you look at the text decide:
    a) how the writer has separated sections of information in the text
    b) how your **skimming** skills can help you sum up the main ideas in each section of information in a few words
    c) what the best way is of organising notes recording the text's main ideas:
        - flow diagram?
        - table?
        - spider diagram?

3   Read the text and make notes (perhaps like the flow diagram opposite) showing its main ideas. For the moment, just order your notes by:
    - writing and numbering each section title
    - leaving spaces between different ideas.

4   Check a friend's notes. Which main ideas, if any, are missing?

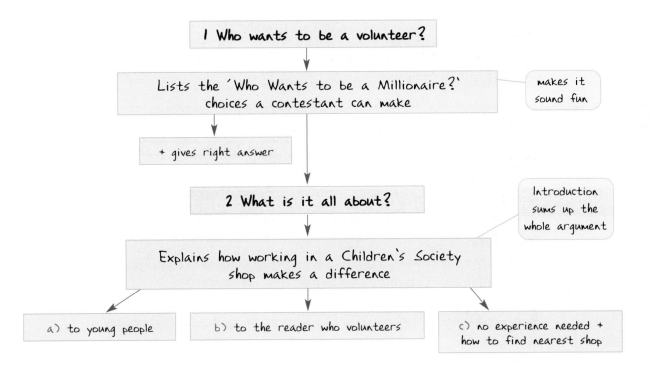

Understanding how ideas are sequenced and developed

The notes you made show the order in which the writer wrote the ideas in the text. Now you are going to investigate:

- how these ideas are developed
- how they follow on from one another
- how they build up to the ending.

5   Study each section of the text in turn and use different colours to add to your notes:

a) numbering and lettering to show what order ideas are in: a), b) etc.

b) arrows to show how ideas link together ⟶

c) a label explaining why the idea in this section adds another reason to persuade the reader to volunteer to work in a Children's Society shop, e.g. *introduction – sums up what The Children's Society want you to do.*

6   The main point of each section is given in its first sentence. The rest of the section is used to develop that idea. For each section in turn decide which of these the writer used to develop the main point:

A   Further detail, e.g. *You don't need any previous experience.*

B   An example, e.g. *sort and price a range of donated goods and stock.*

C   A fact or statistic, e.g. *4 hours… that's the average length of a shift.*

D   A testimony, e.g. *You feel like you're really appreciated.*

7 Look at the final section of the text – its ending.

 a) What is it asking the reader to do?

 b) How has the rest of the text led up to this?

 c) Why is this a good way to end this text?

Understanding the way a persuasion text is built up

Make a flow chart showing the steps you need to take to work out what ideas are in a persuasion text and how they are put together.

8.2   Comparing the style of non-fiction texts

Objectives:

- *identifying how a text's organisation can be tailored to its purpose*
- *using the correct terminology to discuss a non-fiction text*
- *comparing how different forms of campaign texts are presented*
- *examining how the language of a text can be tailored to its purpose.*

Identifying how a text's organisation suits its purpose

1 Bearing in mind what you have already discovered about the text on page 113, explain how using:

 a) questions as headings

 b) different sections for different topics

 helped the writer achieve their purpose.

2 a) Spend **three minutes skimming** the text on page 114, which is a page from a website.

 b) Then answer the questions in this quiz without looking at the text.

 c) Swap answers with a friend and mark each other's answers.

QUICK QUIZ

A What is the text about?

B Who is its audience?

C Complete this sentence explaining the text's purpose.

 The text tries to _____ readers to _____ and to look at _____.

D List four features used to organise information in the text, e.g. headings.

3 How does each of the features you have listed help readers to do what the website suggests? E.g. *The headings help readers to...*

4 In sixty seconds sum up how you can work out whether the way a text is organised suits its purpose. E.g. *First... the text and decide... Next...*

A

Who wants to be a volunteer?

- [ ] Phone a friend
- [ ] 50/50
- [ ] Ask the audience
- [✓] Volunteer

Volunteering
In a Children's Society shop

What's it all about?

Volunteering in a Children's Society shop for just a few hours a week will really make a difference to your life and to the lives of children and young people.

5 Get out of the house for a while, meet new people or do it for work experience.

You don't need any previous work experience but you do need to ring us now to find out where your local shop is.

Just four hours a week?

10 Four hours passes really quickly when you're busy volunteering – that's the average length of a shift. You could do more or less depending on your availability and the needs of the shop.

What does it involve?

15 We have vacancies to
- sort and price a range of donated goods and stock
- steam or iron clothes
- develop your creativity with window
20   displays
- co-ordinate shop rotas
- serve customers and use the till.

If you have an interest in antiques, books, music or fashion, then we also have
25 specialist roles to fill. We'll give you all the training you need for whatever role you undertake.

Who are The Children's Society?

The Children's Society works with 40,000 children and their families throughout the
30 country in over 100 projects. Through the funds raised by our network of 120 shops, we are able to reach out to help children and families in some of the country's most deprived areas.

35 As an organisation that believes in social justice, we reach out to children and young people who need our help, regardless of race or religion.

What do I get out of it?

Being part of the team in our charity shop
40 can give you much more than you put in. Look at what some of our volunteers say...

'You feel like you're really appreciated for what you do.'

'I get a real sense of achievement – and it
45 *gets me out of the house.'* Joy, Bristol

I've now got references and work experience to put on my CV.'

'Everyone's very supportive – I can't believe how much more confident I've become.'
50 Steph, Manchester

What next?

Call Judith on our Freephone number between 9 a.m. and 5 p.m.

0800 980 8524

or leave a message at any time.

B

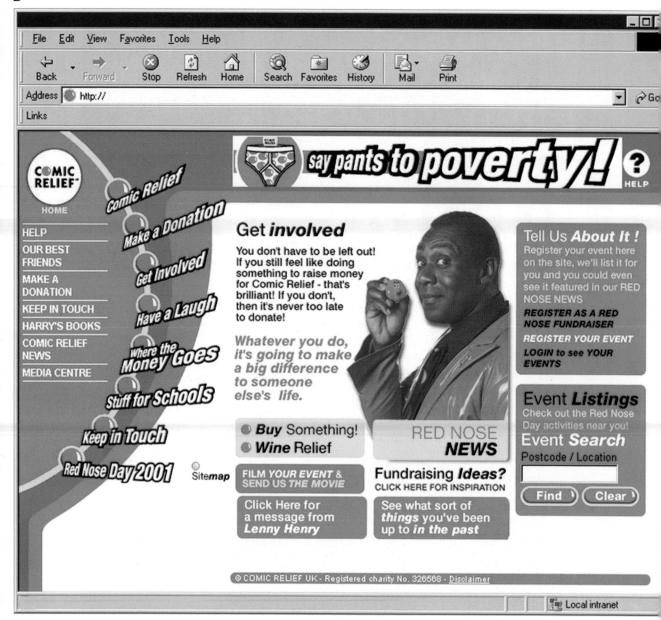

 Identifying the way texts are tailored to suit their purpose

Looking at the form of a campaign text

Since text **A** is a leaflet and text **B** is a website, the amount of time readers will spend looking at each text and the way in which they can respond to it leads writers to craft these texts in different ways.

5 **a)** Compare the way the two texts look, using a table like the one below. The six questions in the box below will help you work out the effect of what you are noticing.

Questions to ask yourself about each visual feature in a media text
1 What is the main idea or subject? E.g. *A picture of... Only colours for...*
2 What ideas are suggested by the colours, font or the way the people, animals etc., are shown? E.g. *Shocking pink is eye-catching but warm and...*
3 Where is it?
4 How big is it?
5 What style is it? E.g. *photograph, cartoon, italics, handwriting?*
6 How is a reader likely to react to it?

Feature	Text A	Text B
Use of colours	white, black writing on a shocking pink...	
Use of pictures	None	Small
Use of fonts, highlighting...		

b) Explain what your table shows, and suggest reasons why the choices writers made suit the way the text is published. E.g. *Both texts use colour. The whole of text **A** is black and white text written on a shocking pink background. This makes it very eye-catching so people will want to pick up the leaflet and read it. Text **B** looks very different because…*

 Looking at the language used in a persuasive text
6 The table below shows some of the language features writers use when they want to persuade readers. Brainstorm any other features they can use and give examples, e.g. *Humour because it appeals to...*

Language feature	Example
• promises or boasts	*'Whatever you do it will make a big difference...'*
• praise	*'That's brilliant!'*
• emotive language	*'the country's most **deprived** areas'*
• appeal to our worries, fears etc.	*'You don't have to be left out'* (appeals to our fear of being left out).
• verbs: Active and imperative	*'**Buy** something!' '**Click** here'*
• adjectives	*'a **big** difference'*
• adverbs	*'If you **still** feel like doing something'*

7   Try to explain why each of the language features listed on page 115 will help persuade readers, e.g. *Promises like this will work because readers want to feel they will definitely get something good out of making the effort to respond.*

WS 8   **a)** Make a tick chart for the two texts and search through them counting how many examples of each of the language features listed on page 115 are used.

	Text A	Text B
Promises or boasts Praise Emotive language		

b) Compare the results of your tick chart and work out the difference between the way language is used in the two texts. E.g. *More... in text...*

9   As you think about
   - the different purpose of each text
   - the media it is published in (leaflet versus website)

discuss how the way each text is presented and written suits its purpose and the time readers will spend reading the leaflet or website, e.g. *Readers will spend longer reading text A so it is worth packing more... especially as the writer wants readers to...*

Preparing to investigate different persuasive texts

10   Make a mind map showing what you should think about when you are investigating how well a persuasive text suits its purpose and audience.

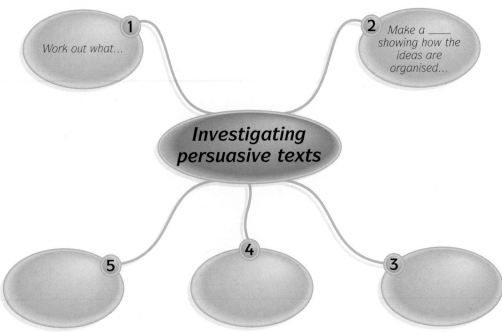

1   *Work out what...*

2   *Make a _____ showing how the ideas are organised...*

Investigating persuasive texts

5

4

3

8.3   Planning a well-argued persuasive text

Objectives:
- *planning a persuasive text*
- *developing ideas and lines of thinking in a text*
- *finding and using different ways to validate an argument*
- *expanding your range of link words and phrases.*

 Planning a persuasive text

You are going to write a leaflet persuading people to take part in a sponsored bike ride in a park near you on 3rd July at 10.00 a.m. to raise money for The Children's Society.

 1   Copy and complete this tick chart, as you investigate text **A** to discover what the main features of a campaign leaflet are:

Feature in campaign leaflets	Tick box	Examples
• an opening statement	✓	lines 1-4
• good reasons and arguments		
• strong positive language		
• draws the reader in by sounding friendly		
• written in present tense		
• personal pronouns		
• facts		
• testimonies		
• persuasive words		
• active verbs		
• a variety of sentence structures		

2   Now make a list of presentational features a leaflet can have (you may add some that were not used in **A**), e.g. *Headings in… Pictures…*

Writing well-thought-through arguments WS

To persuade readers to take part you need strong arguments that:

- give them reasons for wanting to join in, e.g. *It will be fun...*
- help them overcome worries and any arguments they have for not taking part, e.g. *You don't have to be very fit to take part.*

3 **a)** Make a list of all the benefits of taking part in the sponsored cycle ride.

   b) Make a second list of all the possible reasons readers may have for not wanting to take part.

4 **a)** Then work out the arguments you need to put in your leaflet to overcome reasons for not taking part.

   b) Think of ways to back up your argument: facts, testimonies, etc.

   Use a thinking frame like the one below to note your ideas.

Reasons for not taking part	Argument for taking part	Backed up by
Don't know about: what is happening... Surrey	saying when, where	3rd July 10.00 a.m. Richmond Park,
What is in it for me?	It will be fun because...	quotation from...
I'm worried: Am I fit enough? What if...?		

5 Group together information and ideas that will go in each of the six (or more) paragraphs in your leaflet. As you make a plan:

- think about the order in which your arguments should be used, e.g. *start with all the reasons for taking part first, then...*
- make sure that you lead up to your ending effectively, e.g:

Plan

Paragraphs

1 Introduction: sum up...

2 Explain...

6 Remind yourself of the sort of headings used in text **A** on page 113 and how they are connected with what is in the section beneath. Then write a similar list of headings for your leaflet.

7   Below is part of one student's leaflet. Decide what link words or phrases could be used in the blank spaces so that the arguments are clear.

> Taking part in a sponsored bike ride _____ the whole family can have some fun. You don't have to be extremely fit _____ the course is only 5 km. There are plenty of refreshment points _____ that you can drink enough water as you cycle. _____ you or your children feel tired or unwell _____ there will be First Aid...

8   List other link words or phrases you can use to emphasise reasoning.

9   As you write your leaflet you will need to take care to:

a) Concentrate on the positive – avoid emphasising possible problems.
  • How could the student above re-write the second and last sentences so that readers do not notice the problem so much? e.g *The course is suitable for people at all levels of fitness – it is only...*

b) Vary the way you back up your points and give reasons which will overcome any possible objection.
  • What else could the writer add to the highlighted part of the second and last sentences to overcome worries in the readers' minds?

c) Use the link words and phrases you listed to emphasise your reasoning. This will help make your writing more persuasive.
  • Write two more sentences to end this paragraph underlining the link words and phrases you use.

10   Use what you have learned as you write your leaflet.

Writing well-argued persuasive texts

11   Draw a ladder and, starting at the bottom rung, write the different steps you need to take to plan and write a well-argued persuasive text.

NEXT:

AFTER THAT...

THEN...

FIRST WORK OUT REASONS FOR READERS DOING WHAT THEY ARE ASKED

8.4 Writing persuasively

Objectives:
- *drafting a text*
- *positioning subordinate clauses*
- *varying the structure of sentences within paragraphs*
- *using the active or passive voice to suit your purpose.*

During this section you are going to practise re-drafting your leaflet to make it even more persuasive.

Positioning information in a sentence to give it impact

1 Read the student's writing below. As you study the first two sentences decide which information has the most impact and which the least. Why is this?

> Richmond Park, which is well known for its beautiful scenery and wildlife, provides an ideal setting for The Children's Society Cyclathon. By using only the car-free cycle paths, the course has been designed to be both safe and fun. The whole family, from toddlers on their trikes to grandparents on their shoppers, can enjoy raising money together. So get on your bikes and improve a child's future! There's nothing to worry about.
>
> Refreshment stops *will be passed by you at the end of every kilometre. Fully qualified First-Aiders will be available to help any injured riders. Broken chains *will be fixed by mechanics for free.

* these are both examples of passive verbs

It is a useful trick to put the information you want readers to notice most at the beginning of your sentence but to place information you do not want a reader to really notice at the end.

2 How could you re-draft the first and third sentences in the example so that the information highlighted is:
   a) emphasised?
   b) less noticeable? (You can change the wording if you need to.)

3 Now work with a friend. Choose two sentences in each other's leaflets where moving clauses to emphasise them or make them less noticeable will make the sentence more persuasive. Re-write those sentences.

Varying sentences and verbs to emphasise your ideas

4   Read out loud the first paragraph of the student's writing opposite.
    a) Which sentences have most pace? Which have least? Why is this?
    b) Which of the last two sentences should have most emphasis?
    Where can you move it so that readers will notice it more?

5   Scan your leaflet using one colour to tick your simple sentences and
    another to tick your complex sentences. Then check the following:
    a) Are there any paragraphs with only one type of sentence? Have you
    used questions? Exclamations? All simple sentences? All complex?
    b) Do your complex sentences always begin the same way (*for instance,
    with a verb ending in -ing?*) or have you varied the way you organise
    your sentences?

Remember you can begin sentences with:
- a connective   **As** *you cycle you will enjoy…* **While**…
- a verb   **Cycling** *through one of London's…*
- description   **Successful** *runners…*

   c) Should you change any sentences to give them a faster pace?
   d) Is the most important sentence being emphasised? How can you
   change your text to make sure the right information is going to be
   noticed?

6   Read the student's second paragraph and decide:
    a) which information is emphasised in each of the sentences
    b) which sentences have more energy
    c) whether active or passive verbs have been used in each of the
    sentences.

7   Re-write the second paragraph changing verbs in each sentence so that:
    a) in the first and third sentences the subject is emphasised
    b) in the second sentence the object of the sentence is emphasised.

8   Ring any sentence in your leaflet where changing verbs from passive to
    active will give it more energy or emphasise important information better.

9   Now use what you have learned as you re-draft your leaflet.
    - Use a variety of sentence structures.
    - Emphasise the most important information.

Improving persuasive texts

10 Read your friend's work and underline six places where:
    - the type of sentences used is varied
    - the right information is emphasised either because of the sentence
    structure or the writer's use of active or passive verbs.

Reading assignment

This test is 40 minutes long.

- *You should spend the first 5–10 minutes reading the leaflet and questions carefully before you start writing your answers.*
- *Looking at the marks for each question should help you to judge how much to write for each answer.*

Is your name really Mum?

Of course you love him, you're his mother.
But don't you wish you could go back to being Kate,
Jacqui or Laura or whatever your real name is just for a few
hours each day? Here at Oxfam, we can help you do just that,
and to use what you've learnt as a parent: juggling your time,
planning ahead, encouraging, nurturing, motivating. All our
positions are unpaid and will stretch you, but then you're
used to that, aren't you? As a volunteer in one of our
many shops in London and across the south, you'll
get the flexibility to work the hours to fit round your
busy family, the opportunity to gain confidence, the
support to learn and develop, and the chance to
plug those gaps in your CV. For more details and
an information pack, call Kerry, Julian or Carolyn
on 01703 780333, or fill in your details overleaf
and post to Oxfam Volunteering, FREEPOST,
Southampton, SO16 4WG.

Get your real name back.

Oxfam

Volunteer for all our futures

1   In what order do the following arguments appear in this leaflet?

    A   Volunteering to help Oxfam will give you the chance to be you again.

    B   Being a mum can make you feel like you have lost sight of the real you.

    C   Working for Oxfam will help you gain or update skills for your CV.

    D   You can use your parenting skills to help Oxfam.

    [1 mark]

2   Explain two ways in which you can recognise the intended audience for this leaflet.

    [2 marks]

3   Which worries that the intended audience may have, does the writer try to overcome in the first two sentences?

    [2 marks]

4   Re-read the sentence that begins on line 4. How has the writer organised the sentence to emphasise who is best to help the reader?

    [1 mark]

5   How has the writer made sure that the target audience will feel that Oxfam really understands and values them?

    You should comment on:

    • the choice of picture
    • headings
    • arguments that the writer uses
    • words and phrases the writer uses.

    [12 marks]

6   Why is the phrase 'Get your real name back' an effective way to end this text?

    [2 marks]

The Year 7 English test will help you and your teacher see how your reading and writing skills have developed in Year 7 since you took your English SAT at the end of Year 6. It will also show you which skills you are good at and where you need to be stronger, helping you to improve your skills for the Year 8 test, the Year 9 SATs and beyond.

There are two test papers. One paper assesses your reading skills, and the other your writing skills. This section explains what is involved in each test, and what you have to do. It also provides:

● diagnostic tests, which show you where your strengths and weaknesses are, and what you need to do to improve your skills

● practice tests, which help you become familiar with the kind of texts, questions and timing you will meet in the actual tests, so that you will be fully prepared for them.

The reading paper

The texts

The reading paper may contain two, three or four pieces of text.

They will come from a variety of text-types, such as:

● *an extract from a novel or short story*

● *a poem*

● *a piece of information text*

● *a piece of literary non-fiction, such as travel writing.*

The different texts will be linked by a theme or common subject, for example, holidays or hobbies.

There will be an introduction to the texts, including information about:

● *the theme or subject that links the texts*

● *the source of each text – who wrote it and where it came from*

● *the background to the texts. This is particularly important if the text is a short extract from a longer text such as a novel or play.*

The questions

The reading paper contains questions that will test your reading skills, focusing on five key areas.

1   Identifying information or ideas and quoting from the text when required.

2   Working out meanings that are implicit. That means you have to 'read between the lines' of the text to try and work out what is meant. You will need to quote from the text when required.

3 Explaining the structure of texts, for example, how different parts relate to each other, or how the author has used grammar and different kinds of sentences to affect the meaning.

4 Commenting on the writer's choice and use of language.

5 Explaining the overall meaning and effect of a text, and how it affects you as a reader.

To test these skills in the reading paper, different types of questions are asked, including:

- questions that carry only 1 mark and require short answers. This type of question may:
  a) be multiple choice, where you simply tick your choice of answer
  b) ask you to copy a word or phrase from the text to show that you have understood its meaning
- questions that may be worth 2, 3, 4 or 5 marks.

The number of marks available and the space you are given for writing your answer will give you a clue as to how much time you should spend on a question. To help you, 5-mark questions will usually have a series of bullet points. Write about each bullet point to help you structure your answer and make sure it is complete.

Marks

The reading paper is worth 50 marks overall. These marks are divided between the five key reading skills explained above. Within the 50 marks, 10 are given to questions which test your grammatical understanding, for example, about the effects of different sentence structures, or how punctuation helps indicate the meaning in a text.

Giving the best answers to the questions

When answering questions on reading, it is important that you:

- **do exactly what you are asked**. For example, if you are told to copy something from the text, you will get no marks if you put it in your own words.
- **answer the question that is asked**. Make sure that you only include material that answers the question. Including any other material will waste your time, and waste space in your answer book.
- **use textual detail whenever you are told**. Make sure that you use direct quotations if you are commenting on language use or grammar.
- **respond to *all* the prompts** (such as bullet points) in a question, if any are given.
- **complete all the questions in the time allowed**. Plan your time carefully, but if you are running out of time, make sure that you attempt as many questions with high marks as you can.

Using your time carefully

The reading paper lasts for 1 hour and 15 minutes. In addition, you are given an extra 15 minutes to read through the texts before you look at the questions. Use the full 15 minutes reading time to get an overall idea of what the texts are about, and also to:

- think about the type of text each one is, and what that means. For example, how much expression of opinion does there seem to be in a non-fiction text?
- note anything which you find difficult to understand so that you can return to it later
- identify striking or original examples of language use
- think about the effect each text has on you, and what causes the effect. For example, the subject matter could shock you or the style of writing could be humorous and make you laugh.

The writing paper

The tasks

There are two questions on the writing paper:

- *the major task, which is worth 30 marks. It should take 40 minutes and your response should be detailed and wide ranging; for example, a complete story, letter or article.*
- *the minor task, which is worth 20 marks. It should take 25 minutes and be a shorter, more focused response, for example, just the opening of a story or a description of one place, person or object.*

When marking your writing paper the marker will look for a number of different qualities. The major and minor tasks are marked slightly differently and the marker will look for different skills in each.

The major task

The four skills assessed in the major task are:

1 **How you structure and punctuate sentences.** For example, do you use full stops and capital letters, commas and other punctuation marks accurately? Do you vary your sentences so that they are not always simple (*The cat sat on the mat.*) but are sometimes compound (*The cat sat on the mat and the dog entered the room.*) or complex (*As the dog entered the room, the cat was sitting on the mat.*)? (Marks are given out of 5.)

2 **How you organise paragraphs and ensure that the complete piece of writing 'hangs together'.** For example, does a narrative follow a straightforward chronological sequence or, if you use a more complicated structure (such as flashback), does it make sense to the reader? If you are writing an argument, do your ideas follow a logical sequence so that the reader finds it hard to disagree with you? (Marks are given out of 5.)

3 **The overall impact of your writing on the reader.** This means how well your writing meets its **purpose** and how well it suits its **audience**. In other words, if it is a story, does it include interesting characters and believable events in a well-described setting? If it is a letter to a friend, have you used appropriate vocabulary and is the content interesting? (Marks are given out of 15.)

4 **The accuracy of your spelling.** You must show that you can spell difficult or less common words correctly to gain a high mark. (Marks are given out of 5.)

The minor task

The three skills assessed in the minor task are:

1 **Your choice and use of vocabulary.** You will gain more marks for using a wide vocabulary, even if you mis-spell some words. (Marks are given out of 4.)

2 **How you structure and punctuate sentences and organise paragraphs.** See major task points 1 and 2 above. (Marks are given out of 4.)

3 **The overall impact of your writing on the reader.** See major task point 3 above. (Marks are given out of 12.)

Why are the major and minor tests marked differently?

The reason for marking the major and minor tasks differently is because the two tasks ask you to do different things.

- You need to give a longer response to the major task. The marker will look separately at how you create sentences and organise paragraphs and how accurate your spelling is within this longer response.

- You need to give a shorter response to the minor task. Sometimes you will be asked to write only a few paragraphs, for example, only three. This means that paragraph organisation is less important, but your choice and use of vocabulary is more important.

Giving the best answers to questions

When answering writing questions, it is important that you:

- Write in the correct form. For example, if you are told to write a **description**, do not write a **story**.
- Write for the given reader. For example, if you are told to write one piece for a teenage friend and another for an unknown adult, you should use more formal language and grammar in the second piece.
- Cover the content. For example, if you are told to include certain information or events, or to start or finish in a given way, you will lose marks if you do not follow the instructions.
- Interest the reader. For example, use as wide a range of vocabulary as possible, and vary sentence structures and length of paragraphs.
- Show a high level of technical accuracy and neatness. For example, your work must be legible so that whoever is marking it can see that spellings and punctuation are accurate.

Using your time carefully

The time allowed for the writing paper is 1 hour and 15 minutes.
You should spend:

- 40 minutes on the major task
- 25 minutes on the minor task
- 10 minutes at the end, checking all your work for neatness, accuracy and completeness.

Each task is followed by a **planning frame** for you to copy out and make notes in – make sure you leave plenty of space in each of the boxes to write your ideas in. These frames will help you gather together and organise your ideas, and begin to think about the best ways of writing about them. The planning frames are an extremely helpful part of the test, and you may find it helpful to allow the following time for planning and making notes:

- 10 minutes of your major task time
- 5–6 minutes of your minor task time.

Planning your writing will help you produce a piece of writing which is likely to be much better than if you simply start writing straight away.

Using the diagnostic and practice tests

The diagnostic tests

The diagnostic reading and writing tests on pages 130–133 and 134 will help you and your teacher to assess the strengths and weaknesses of your reading and writing skills. It is a slightly shorter and simpler version of the actual test. You may find it helpful to use this test quite near the start of Year 7 to assess how well you can use the skills you learned in Key Stage 2. The results from this test will give you and your teacher a better idea of areas that you need to work on to improve your reading and writing skills during Year 7.

The practice tests

The practice reading and writing tests on pages 135–142 and 143–144 follow the exact format, length and timing of the actual test. You may find it helpful to use this test later in Year 7. The results will show you and your teacher where your reading and writing skills have improved during the year. It will also highlight specific areas of your reading and writing skills that might still be improved before you take the actual test.

Marking the tests and setting targets

Your teacher will mark both the diagnostic tests and the practice tests. You will be given a total mark for each test:

- out of 70 marks for the diagnostic test
- out of 100 marks for the practice test.

Your teacher will be able to tell you a National Curriculum Level in English to which this mark corresponds. This will tell you how much overall progress you are making, as well as your progress in the separate areas of reading and writing, for which your teacher will give you a separate mark. Your teacher will even be able to give you a breakdown of your marks for all the different assessment focuses in reading and writing. This will show you exactly where your strengths and weaknesses are, and will focus on areas that will improve your reading and writing skills throughout Key Stage 3 and beyond.

Diagnostic tests

Reading test

Read the following texts:

> *The first text is taken from **Born Free** by Joy Adamson, the true story of how she and her husband, George, reared a lion cub, Elsa. As she grew older, Elsa developed the remarkable ability to behave almost like a pet with the Adamsons, but to keep her natural instincts in other situations. This extract describes an occasion when Elsa showed both sides of her character.*

On our way home George shot a waterbuck which was standing in the river. Badly hit, it dashed across to the opposite side, followed by Elsa, who splashed unbelievably fast through the deep water. When we arrived at the other bank we found her amongst the river bush, panting, on top
5 of the dead buck. She was very excited and did not allow us to touch her kill. So we decided to return home and leave her to guard it. As soon as we started wading back through the water, she began to follow us, but seemed torn between conflicting impulses: she did not want to be left on the wrong side of the river with her kill, on the other hand she did not
10 want to lose it. Eventually she returned reluctantly to it, but soon made another attempt to cross, only to turn back again but undecidedly. However, by the time we had reached the opposite bank Elsa had made up her mind.

Now we saw her dragging the buck into the water. What was she up to?
15 Surely she could not bring this heavy animal across alone? But Elsa was not going to be defeated. She held the carcase in her mouth and swam with it through the deep water, her head often submerged to get a better grip. She hauled and tugged, pushed and pulled, and when the buck got stuck, pounced on it to get it floating again. Often both disappeared from
20 view and only Elsa's tail or one leg of the buck told us of the struggle that was going on at the bottom of the river. We watched fascinated. After half an hour of strenuous effort, she trailed her quarry proudly through the shallow water near to us. By now she was really exhausted, but her task was not finished yet. After tugging the buck into a little sheltered bay
25 where the current could not carry it away, she looked for a safe hiding-place. The bank here was a solid network of sharp-edged, thorn-hooked doum-palm seedlings, which overhung the steep walls that lined the river; even Elsa could not penetrate this thicket.

We left her with her kill and went back to camp to collect some bush
30 knives and ropes and to have our overdue breakfast. When we returned, we cut a passage through the doum-palm undergrowth to the water's edge and, while Elsa watched the men suspiciously, I slipped a rope noose

over the buck's head. Now all was ready to haul it up the steep bank.
At the first tug Elsa growled and flattened her ears warningly – obviously
35 she thought that her kill was going to be taken away from her. But as soon
as she saw me join in the pulling, she relaxed, and climbed up the bank.
Our combined efforts landed the buck ten feet above the river where the
boys had cut a well protected shady shelter for Elsa and her kill. Now she
realised what we had done for her and it was touching to see her going
40 from one to another of us, rubbing her head and thanking everyone in turn
with a low moan.

> *The second extract is from Robert Westall's novel* **Blitzcat**. *It tells the
> story of a cat who is taken away from her home during the Second
> World War when some of the family that owns her moves to the safety
> of the Dorset countryside. She misses her home, and in particular one
> of the family, who is a fighter pilot; the cat makes up her mind to find
> them again.*

A biggish black she-cat with only a few white hairs, invisible beneath her
chin. It is impossible to understand exactly what was on her mind. But she
was used to having her own way. She did not like noise and upset. She
hated the strange house at Beaminster, full of women and children, tears
5 and tantrums. She hated the smells of sour milk and nappies, and the
toddlers in every room who would not leave her in peace. She hated the
close-packed smells of the Beaminster cats when she went outdoors; cats
who attacked her in defence of their own territory wherever she walked.

And she hated the way her own people no longer had any time to stroke
10 and fuss her. She hated the kitchen scraps she was fed, instead of fresh-
boiled fish. Above all, she hated the new baby.

She was going back to where she'd been peaceful; where she could spend
hours alone, sleeping on the silken coverlet of a sunlit bed in the long
afternoons; where she could go to the kitchen and get fresh fish and milk
15 on demand. Somehow, sure as a homing-pigeon, she knew it was ahead.

More dimly – and this was something no homing-pigeon knew – she
knew her *real* person was ahead; only further off, *much* further off. She
remembered his gentle voice calling her, in the mornings; the tobaccoish
smell of his hand stroking her. She remembered riding about on his
20 shoulder, while his gentle hands caressed her. She remembered the game
in the garden, when he lay hidden in the long grass, and flicked his white
handkerchief while she stalked him. Then she would pounce on him, and
they would roll over and over in mock-fury, until the ecstasy of his
nearness grew too much for her, and she would scamper off, her back
25 twitching with too much pleasure. To stalk again. And the long evenings
by the fire, in his lap, when she would end up lying on her back, paws
in the air, and her head hanging abandoned down his long shins.

Somewhere ahead, there was endless happiness again. And she knew
how to get there.

Now answer these questions

*Questions 1–8 are on the extract from **Born Free***

1 **(a)** In line 2, what do the words *Badly hit, it...* refer to?

[1 mark]

   (b) The writer could have started this sentence, *It was badly hit and...* How is the choice she made more effective than this alternative?

[2 marks]

2 In the first paragraph, Elsa is described as behaving *undecidedly*. Find and copy **two** other phrases from the same paragraph which convey this impression.

[2 marks]

3 **(a)** Why do you think the writer includes two questions at the start of the second paragraph? Give two reasons.

[2 marks]

   (b) Explain the use of the semi-colon in the last sentence of the second paragraph.

[1 mark]

4 What impression of Elsa's actions do you get from:
   (a) the verbs in the sentence *She hauled and tugged... to get it floating again* (lines 18–19)?

[1 mark]

   (b) the adverb *proudly* in line 22?

[1 mark]

5 In the last sentence of the second paragraph, what does the word *even* suggest to you about Elsa?

[1 mark]

6 Why is the breakfast described as *overdue* (line 30)?

[2 marks]

7 What effect is gained by the writer repeating the words *her kill* twice in both the first and the last paragraphs?

[2 marks]

8 Explain as fully as you can what this text tells you about the relationship between Elsa and the humans. You should write about:
   • Elsa's reactions when the waterbuck is wounded
   • how Elsa responds to the men who help get the waterbuck out of the river
   • the meaning of the final sentence.

[5 marks]

Questions 9–16 are on the extract from **Blitzcat**

9 What is the effect of this extract starting with a sentence which has no finite verb?

[2 marks]

10 From paragraph 1, list (i) a *noise* and (ii) an *upset* which the cat does not like.

[2 marks]

11 What is the meaning of the word *close-packed* in line 7?

[2 marks]

12 Comment on the use and effect of the words *sleeping*, *silken* and *sunlit* in line 13.

[3 marks]

13 Why do you think the writer italicises the words *real* and *much* in the fourth paragraph?

[1 mark]

14 What can you say about the structure and effect of the sentence *To stalk again* (line 25)?

[2 marks]

15 From the fourth paragraph, list **three** words which show the affection the cat feels for her missing master.

[3 marks]

16 In this extract, how does the writer convey the cat's unhappiness? You should write about:
- the use of repetition
- the use of lists and detail
- the use of contrast
- the choice of words.

[5 marks]

Writing test

Think back to the texts you read about Elsa the lioness and the blitzcat. Both writers described the animals in such a way that you found out a lot about their characteristics, for example, their determination, as well as their physical qualities and lifestyles.

Write your own description of an animal.

Your finished piece should inform the reader about the animal's appearance, but should also explain some of its characteristics. Before starting to plan, you will need to decide:

- the animal you want to describe – is it domestic or wild? Is it one you have personal knowledge of, or one that you have seen on film or in a book?

- what sort of situation you can put the animal in to bring out its qualities – for example, a dog playing with someone or an elephant charging an enemy.

Remember you are not writing a story: this is a piece which should inform, explain and describe. Before starting to write, you will need to think about:

- the choice of descriptive language which will help your reader picture the animal and understand something about it

- how you will structure your piece – for example, will you start with a description, or with the animal in action?

Copy this planning grid and use it to help you organise your ideas. Don't forget to leave enough space in each of the boxes to include your ideas.

Name or type of animal chosen:		
	Suitable vocabulary to use	Place in structure/ number of paragraphs
Aspect of animal		
Physical features		
Characteristics		
Situation		

Practice tests

Reading test: Fighters

> **REMEMBER:**
> - *The test is 1 hour 15 minutes long, plus 15 minutes' reading time.*
> - *You therefore have 15 minutes to read the texts before answering the questions that follow them.*
> - *There are different types of questions. The spaces for answers and the number of marks indicate how much you need to write.*
> - *Ask your teacher if you are not sure what to do.*

Introduction

Individual people, groups and nations often have disagreements. Sometimes these are quickly sorted out, but at other times they develop into serious fights or battles. We are used to hearing almost every day about wars or terrorist activities. The texts for this reading test are connected by the theme of warfare – actual, fictional and imaginary. The first and third texts are about the two World Wars which took place in the twentieth century, while the second is a poem which uses the image of a terrorist to reflect on human nature.

'A fascinating monster'

This is an extract from *The Making of Me*, a short story by Robert Westall. The story is set in the period after the First World War. It is about a grown man remembering his life as a young boy, and the influence his grandfather had on his upbringing.

Terrorist

This is a poem by Anne Stevenson. She was born and brought up in the USA, but has spent most of her life in England.

Verdun

This is an extract from *The Roses of No Man's Land* by Lyn MacDonald. This book tells the true story of the volunteer nurses who worked behind the battle lines in France during the First World War.

'A fascinating monster'

> The storyteller looks back on his childhood, when his parents often left
> him with other adults when they went off somewhere. He hated being left
> with anyone, but especially with his grandparents. Although his nana was
> kind and jolly, his grandfather was quite different…

My grandfather was not a *person*, like my mum and dad, or my little
round laughing nana. He towered above me, six feet tall. I would sometimes
glance up at him, as one might peer up in awe at a mountainous crag. The
huge nose, the drooping moustache, the drooping mass of wrinkles. Then
5 his eyes would peer down at me, too small, too close together, pale blue,
wild and empty of everything but an everlasting, baffled rage. And my own
eyes would scurry for cover, like a scared rabbit. He never spoke to me,
and I never spoke to him, and thank God my parents never forced me to,
as they would force me sometimes to kiss hairy-chinned old ladies.

10 There were old tales of his violence. How when his second child was born
dead, he ripped the gas-cooker from the wall and threw it downstairs (and
gas-cookers were solid cast-iron then, and weighed a ton). How when he
came home drunk on a Saturday night, Nana and my eleven-year-old
father would hear his step and run to hide in the outside wash-house, till
15 he fell into a drunken sleep before the fire. And then Nana would stealthily
rifle his pockets for the remains of his week's wages, and go straight to
buy the week's shopping before he woke. And when he woke, he would
think he'd lost all his money in his drunken stupor.

But the Great War had done for him. Unlike anybody else I knew, he had a
20 Chest, because he'd been gassed in the trenches. His Chest made
a fascinating symphony of noises at the best of times. So I would listen to
it, rather than the chat round the meal-table. But when he was upstairs in
bed, bad with his Chest, the whole house was silent and doom-laden, and
my parents tiptoed about and talked in whispers.

25 He was also shell-shocked. Nana always had to be careful with the big
black kettle she kept simmering on the hob to make a cup of tea. If it was
allowed to boil, the lid would begin to rattle, making exactly the same noise
as a distant machine-gun. And that would be enough to send him off into
one of his 'dos', when he would imagine he was back in the hell of the
30 trenches and would shout despairing orders, and I would be sent out for
a walk till one of his powders settled him.

They said he had killed an Austrian soldier in a bayonet fight and taken his
cap-badge. I was sometimes allowed to handle the strange square badge,
to keep me quiet. It had a picture in brass of charging infantry-men, and

35 strange, eastern, Hungarian writing. When Granda was *really* bad, he thought the dead Austrian had come back for his badge.

And, above all, he still drank. Perhaps to drown the memories he never spoke of. Oh, the silent agony of waiting to eat Sunday lunch, because of him, at our house; my mother fretting and the painful smell of good roast
40 beef being singed to a crisp in the oven. Every ear cocked for his wavering footsteps. The strange bits of French songs or German marches that he would hum while he pushed his food unwanted round his plate.

Afterwards he would fall asleep with his mouth open. There was never any blackness for me like the blackness of the inside of his mouth.

45 But, while my parents were there, and the Nana I loved, he was just a fascinating monster, a fabulous beast. Safe to watch, like a tiger in a cage.

But being left alone with him…

A dreadful silence always fell. Perhaps he thought he had nothing in his mind fit for a child's ears. And my childish prattle, which so made the
50 other grown-ups laugh, just got on his shell-shocked nerves.

Once, without warning, he clouted me across the ear. I think I wasn't so much hurt as *outraged*. Nobody had ever hit me, except my father twice, and that after plenty of warnings. The unfairness of it made the world reel about me. He told my father, afterwards, that I turned to him with tears in
55 my eyes and said,

'Why did you hit me, grandfather?'

*From **The Making of Me** by Robert Westall*

Terrorist

> In this poem, Anne Stevenson describes something that happens when she
> is sitting at work one day. It makes her think differently about her writing.

One morning I despaired of writing more,
    never any more,
when a swallow swooped in, around and out
    the open door,
5 then in again and batlike to the window,
    against which
beating himself, a suicide in jail,
    he now and then collapsed into
his midnight iridescent combat suit,
10   beautiful white markings on the tail.

Inside his balaclava, all he knew
    was something light and airy he had come from
flattened into something hard and blue.
    Thank God for all those drafts I used to
15 scoop, shove or shovel him to the transom,
    open just enough to let him through.

Off he flew, writing his easy looped
    imaginary line.
No sign of his adventure left behind
20   but my surprise
and his – not fright, though he had
    frightened me, those two
bright high-tech bullets called his eyes.
    What they said was
25 'Fight and fight and fight. No compromise.'

Verdun

The First World War has already lasted for a year and a half, and in northern France the Germans and the Allied Armies of France and Britain are dug into trenches. From time to time, a battle is launched, and thousands of men are killed – many by bullets, shells and gas, others by drowning in water-filled shell-craters – just to win a few yards of mud, or sometimes nothing at all. On both sides, the leaders of the armies are trying to come up with a strategy that will gain victory and bring the misery to an end.

At the beginning of 1916 the Germans were at the zenith of their fortune: Serbia (which had never really mattered much) had been finally overrun. The Russians, torn by the first stirrings of internal strife, were struggling on the Eastern Front. The Allies had abandoned Gallipoli and, still bleeding
5   from huge losses, were unable to budge in the West. It seemed a propitious time to deal a blow that would bring the French to their knees and force Britain to throw in the sponge.

Verdun. They had almost taken it in 1914 but Verdun had held out, as it held out almost until France itself had collapsed under the weight of the
10 Prussian war machine in 1870. Verdun. Like two dogs worrying a bone, France and Germany had been snarling over it at intervals for a thousand years. Verdun. A citadel town, manned by a permanent garrison, surrounded by impregnable forts built on encircling ridges that were in themselves natural defences. Verdun. A bastion, a bulwark, the place
15 above all others which the French army would rush to defend.

That they should rush to defend it was the cornerstone of the German strategy. It was not part of von Falkenhayn's original plan to take Verdun itself. But the city lay deep in a salient and if the French army could be lured into it, under the guns ranged round it on three sides, it could be
20 blown out of existence. Successive waves of reinforcements could be pulverized in their turn, and with very little expenditure of her own resources of manpower, Germany could bleed the French white. Then, as von Falkenhayn gloated in anticipation, with 'England's best sword knocked out of her hand' the Allies would be forced to sue for peace.
25 Verdun would be the bait. In January the Germans prepared to set the trap.

*From **The Roses of No Man's Land** by Lyn MacDonald*

Questions 1–9 are on **'A fascinating monster'**

1   How did the storyteller's nana sometimes have to get money for her shopping?

[2 marks]

2   Which of the following best describes the storyteller's feelings about his grandfather?
   (a) He loved him.
   (b) He felt sorry for him.
   (c) He was scared of him.
   (d) He hated him.

[1 mark]

3   What does the word *symphony* suggest in the third paragraph?

[3 marks]

4   What does this sentence mean:
   There was never any blackness for me like the blackness of the inside of his mouth (paragraph 7)?

[2 marks]

5   Explain why capital (upper case) letters are used for:
   (a) Great War (paragraph 3)
   (b) Chest (paragraph 3).

[2 marks]

6   What is unusual about this sentence, and what is its effect?
   Safe to watch, like a tiger in a cage (paragraph 8).

[2 marks]

7   Why, in the last paragraph, is the word *outraged* italicised?

[1 mark]

8   **(a)** How do the storyteller's parents expect him to behave?
   (b) How do you know this?

[2 marks]

9   What overall impression of the storyteller's grandfather do you get from this extract?
   You should write about:
   • how the storyteller feels about him
   • how others react to him
   • the reasons for his behaviour
   • whether you feel any sympathy for him or not.

[5 marks]

Questions 10–15 are on **Terrorist**

10 **(a)** Explain in your own words the feeling described by the writer
    in the first two lines of the poem.

    (b) What is the reason for this feeling?

[2 marks]

11 Comment on the choice and effect of *swooped* in line 3.

[3 marks]

12 At the start of the second stanza, what is the meaning of the lines

> *all he knew*
> *was something light and airy he had come from*
> *flattened into something hard and blue.*

[1 mark]

13 What is the connection between the first two lines of the last
    stanza and the first two lines of the first stanza?

[2 marks]

14 Look again at the last line of the poem. Explain the message
    the writer takes from the swallow's eyes.

[2 marks]

15 This poem is an extended metaphor through which the swallow
    is seen as a freedom fighter.

    Comment on how the writer uses this to communicate meaning
    effectively to the reader. You should write about:

    ● the impact of individual words and phrases
    ● how the overall metaphor is appropriate to the meaning of the poem
    ● the effect the poem has on you.

[5 marks]

Questions 16–21 are on **Verdun**

16 At the beginning of 1916, the German army was (pick one answer):

    (a) weakened by huge losses
    (b) struggling on the Eastern Front
    (c) enjoying very good fortune
    (d) about to overrun Serbia.

[1 mark]

17 Explain the effectiveness of these words used at the end of
    the first paragraph: *a blow that would bring the French to
    their knees and force Britain to throw in the sponge*.

[3 marks]

18 Why do you think the writer repeats the single-word sentence
    Verdun four times in the second paragraph?

[3 marks]

19 An important part of von Falkenhayn's strategy was that (pick one answer):

(a) France would defend Verdun

(b) the Germans should capture Verdun

(c) the English army would be defeated at Verdun

(d) the German army should retreat from Verdun.

[1 mark]

20 Look at the sentence in the third paragraph *Then, as von Falkenhayn gloated in anticipation, with 'England's best sword knocked out of her hand' the Allies would be forced to sue for peace.*

(a) Why do you think some of the words are placed inside inverted commas?

(b) What is the effect of including these words in the text?

[2 marks]

21 How does the writer build up a sense of tension in this text? You should write about:

• the content

• the structure, including sentence patterns

• the use of language.

[5 marks]

Writing test: Fighters

> **Major task:** you should spend about 40 minutes answering this question.

Is it right to fight?

Two young people of your age have been learning about the First World War in a history lesson. Afterwards, they have a discussion about whether it is right to go to war and fight for your country.

One of them thinks that you should be prepared to fight and die for your country to protect its independence and to guard the lives of your family, friends and loved ones.

The other believes that because war causes so much devastation to people and damage to our world, it is never justified.

Write the conversation they have, set out as a playscript, in which each tries to persuade the other to change their point of view.

> **REMEMBER TO INCLUDE:**
> * *clear statements of each young person's viewpoint*
> * *persuasive language, to try to change the other person's mind*
> * *appropriate stage directions, such as indications of tone of voice, movements or gestures.*

[30 marks]

Planning

Before you begin to write your playscript, copy this frame and use it to gather together and organise your ideas. Don't forget to leave enough space in each of the boxes to include your ideas.

Is it right to fight?: Planning frame

Person A – name?		Person B – name?	
What A believes	Reasons	What B believes	Reasons
What sort of person A is	How this comes across	What sort of person B is	How this comes across
Words or phrases A might use		Words or phrases B might use	
Will A change his/her mind? Why (not)?		Will B change his/her mind? Why (not)?	
Notes on the content/structure of the conversation			
How to begin	The main part		How to end

Minor task: you should spend about 25 minutes answering this question.

Beyond repair

You are planning to write a story – it may be a mystery story, a horror story or a story about an everyday situation. You have decided to start your story with a description of a ruined building. This description will set the atmosphere for the events which happen later.

Write three paragraphs which describe the ruined building.

> REMEMBER:
> - *You should not go on to the story – just write the opening description of the building.*
> - *The description should establish an atmosphere – for example, mysterious, sad or frightening.*
> - *You will need to choose vocabulary carefully so that you create the effect you want.*

[20 marks]

Planning

Before you begin to write your description, copy this frame and use it to gather together and organise your ideas. Don't forget to leave enough space in each of the boxes to include your ideas.

Beyond repair: Planning frame

Type of story the description is introducing:		
Atmosphere you want to establish:		
What sort of building is it?		
What has damaged it?		
What are the ruined building's striking features?		
Words and phrases to use:		
Paragraph plan – content		
Paragraph 1	Paragraph 2	Paragraph 3